THE
STAR-SPANGLED
BANNER

Also by Michael Ruby

Poetry Books

The Mouth of the Bay (2019, BlazeVOX [books])
American Songbook (2013, Ugly Duckling Presse)
Memories, Dreams and Inner Voices, a trilogy (2012, Station Hill Press)
Compulsive Words (2010, BlazeVOX)
The Edge of the Underworld (2010, BlazeVOX)
Window on the City (2006, BlazeVOX)
At an Intersection (2002, Alef Books)

Poetry Ebooks

Titles & First Lines (2018, Mudlark)
Close Your Eyes (2018, Argotist Online)
Inner Voices Heard Before Sleep (2011, Argotist Online)
Fleeting Memories (2008, Ugly Duckling)

Edited Books

Piece of Cake by Bernadette Mayer and Lewis Warsh, co-edited
with Sam Truitt (2019, Station Hill)
Eating the Colors of a Lineup of Words: The Early Books of Bernadette Mayer,
co-edited with Sam Truitt (2015, Station Hill)
Washtenaw County Jail and Other Writings by David Herfort (2005, Xlibris)

THE
STAR-SPANGLED
BANNER

Michael Ruby

Station Hill Press

Published by Station Hill Press, the publishing project of the Institute for Publishing Arts, Inc., 120 Station Hill Road, Barrytown, NY 12507, New York, a not-for-profit, tax-exempt organization [501(c)(3)].

Online catalogue: www.stationhill.org
e-mail: publishers@stationhill.org

Cover and interior design: Sherry Williams

Fourteen of the poems in this book were first published in a chapbook exchanged with members of Dusie Kollektiv 5 in Zurich in 2011. Twenty-seven other poems were first published in the print magazines *Greetings* and *Poems by Sunday*, and in the ezines *Barzakh*, *Boog City*, *EOAGH*, *mprsnd*, *Otoliths*, *Truck* and *Unlikely Stories*. Thanks to the editors of those publications.

Library of Congress Cataloging-in-Publication Data

Names: Ruby, Michael (Michael Handler), author.
Title: The Star-spangled banner / Michael Ruby.
Identifiers: LCCN 2020023774 | ISBN 9781581771992 (paperback)
Subjects: LCSH: Political poetry, American. | United States—Politics and
    government--21st century--Poetry. | Star-spangled banner (Song)—
Poetry.
    | LCGFT: Poetry.
Classification: LCC PS3618.U325 S73 2020 | DDC 811/.6--dc23
LC record available at https://lccn.loc.gov/2020023774

Manufactured in the United States of America

CONTENTS

For Jimi Hendrix and Jasper Johns

From a Red 2001 Standard Diary

O Tuesday September 11 say Sunny and blue, can a day hard to excavate
    you only two days later. see Primary day in New York.
By Russ leafleting the near P.S. 321 dawn's as I took the girlies early to
    their schools. light Was there a blast
What on the way home? so Louisa calls: proudly "Turn on the TV." we The
    plane's hitting hailed the second tower.
At Sam calls. the I go up to the roof twilight's with binoculars, last
    describing what I see gleaming over the phone.

Whose Huge plumes of black smoke broad arc over us in Brooklyn. stripes
    I look through binoculars and at the burning floors. bright "I don't see
    how anyone stars can survive above the burning."
Through Back and forth the from the roof to the TV. perilous Why is the
    smoke suddenly going *down*? fight "Did it collapse?"
O'er I yelled to the next rooftop. the The guy nodded. ramparts I lay down
    on the roof and cried. we Thousands dead. People we knew. watched
    Phone calls poured in:
Were Maude, Billy.... so Louisa's walking home gallantly from the Upper
    East Side streaming with Janet.

And Where's Mom & Eli? the Debra's worried about Michele. rocket's My
    boss Jesse says red the newspaper's moved to South Brunswick glare
    and I can't get there.
The TV, TV, TV. bombs No lunch. bursting On the roof, in smoke obscured
    Lower Manhattan. air I left Mom and Eli
Gave to get Charlotte at 3. proof Charlotte and I got Emily and Natalie.
    through The girlies were worried about Hudson River Park. the TV, TV,
    TV. night Phone, phone, phone
That for what seemed like days. our Total hypnotism and paralysis. flag
    Maybe I went to the roof. was I was basically needed still to man the
    phones there (for the family).

O Louisa got home at 5 say from her endless walk. does After that point, that the
day is a pure jumble star of lying on the bed spangled watching TV, banner
talking on the phone, yet listening to Louisa wave talk on the phone.
O'er I must have talked the to Mark countless times. land Talked a long time
to Sandy of (Liz called the and Louisa never told me). free Bush's speech
infuriated me,
And it had nothing for us the here in New York. home Another night of of
sleeping in the study the to avoid the mosquitoes brave in our bedroom.

★

O world say words can need you retreat see light
By will the tree dawn's promise early ignorance light world
What ails so full proudly unattractive we destroyers hailed love
At one the grass twilight's deception last thought gleaming water

Whose money broad recede stripes sky and others bright distance
    stars weep
Through rocks the sea perilous germ fight ease
O'er mountains the sky ramparts charm we creators watched others
Were alive so full gallantly refusing streaming tears

And others the sun rocket's imprecise red inside glare outside
The storm bombs kill bursting membranes in space air lives
Gave money proof oppressive through water the road night ease
That man our fault flag errors was beautiful still alive there waiting

O world say words does work that man star recedes spangled water banner
    lie yet uncertain wave love
O'er mountains the structures land hard of earth the signs free race
And others the people home peace of earth the time brave life

★

O unconscious say spineless can oracles you perspire see Bremen
By Turkey the lemon dawn's operation early smorgasbord light alright
What peaceloving so ominous proudly argumentative we eagles hailed topsoil
By oceans the makeshift twilight's magazines last person gleaming seagulls

Whose potential broad buttocks stripes licked and mortified bright lemons
    stars alive
Through vanquished the meager perilous bacon fight hives
O'er Tokyo the perpetual ramparts daybook we elevated watched basins
Were partial so hybrid gallantly pupils streaming lies

And Morrison the manifold rocket's song red tuna glare believer
The perfect bombs alert bursting fulsome in time air fort
Gave mockery proof instantaneous through peels the message night harps
That military our nightmare flag past was Emmental still beakers there
    broken

O arrange say Rome does smell that liminal star fucker spangled holster
    banner soup yet Tabasco wave Mommy
O'er pizza the medium land passion of alphabets the lemon free dikes
And people the performance home bakery of extraterrestrial the melanin
    brave tuba

Signs on the Post-9/11 Commute to Work

O AMBULANCE ZONE say 8 AM-11 AM THURS can NO PARKING ANYTIME
you COFFEE TEA SODA BEER see DRIVE THRU
By WEST BKLYN-QUNS EXPY the YIELD dawn's BUYING OR SELLING A
HOME? early SAY NO TO DRUGS BUT YES TO RUGS light 278 WEST
STATEN ISLAND
What LEAVING BROOKLYN FUHGEDDABOUTIT so NO CAMERAS proudly
FINES DOUBLED FOR SPEEDING IN WORK ZONES we FIRE HOSE
VALVES hailed E-Z PASS CASH
At REPORT SUSPICIOUS ACTIVITY the URGENT MESSAGE WHEN
FLASHING twilight's POW-MIA MEMORIAL HWY last SNOW
EMERGENCY ROUTE gleaming BUS LANE

Whose MERGE broad YIELD stripes DR ML KING JR EXPWY and WEST
SHORE EXPWY bright OUTERBRIDGE CROSSING stars NYSDOT SIGN
UNDER TEST
Through LOCAL TRUCK ROUTE the ARTHUR KILL RD perilous EMERGENCY
STOPPING ONLY fight KOREAN WAR VETS PKWY NORTH
O'er LAST EXIT IN NEW YORK the RESTRICTED ON BRIDGE ramparts
STATEN ISLAND ANIMAL RECEIVING FACILITY we ROADWAY UNDER
VIDEO SURVEILLANCE watched WELCOME TO NEW JERSEY
Were NO TURNS so SAVIOR gallantly NEW JERSEY TURNPIKE NEXT RIGHT
streaming INTERSTATE 95

And DO NOT BACK UP the CARS ONLY rocket's NO STOPPING EXCEPT FOR
REPAIRS red OFFICIAL USE ONLY glare NO TURNS
The E-Z PASS NO CASH bombs TO SOUTH 1 bursting FINES DOUBLED in
NO STOPPING OR STANDING air ALL TURNS
Gave MILLTOWN NORTH BRUNSWICK NEW BRUNSWICK proof SHOPPING
CENTER through RIGHT LANE MUST TURN RIGHT the NO TURNS night
JERSEY AVE. EXIT ½ MILE
That SOUTH 1 our CARNEVALE ITALIANO flag TREES ARE TREATED WITH
NOXIOUS SPRAY was LANE ENDS still NO ATM FEE there A CLEAN
COMMUNITY

O NO STOPPING OR STANDING say CHUTNEY MANOR BANQUET HALL does
    DRUG-FREE SCHOOL ZONE that NORTHUMBERLAND WAY star
    SANDHILL RD spangled ENTERING TWP OF SO. BRUNSWICK banner
    MR. GOODLUBE yet MONMOUTH MOBILE PARK wave EXXON
    125.9 137.9 148.9
O'er BURRITO ROYALE the ISLAMIC SOCIETY OF CENTRAL JERSEY land
    PET SMART of RESIDENCE INN MARRIOTT the PRINCETON EXECUTIVE
    CENTER free BOY SCOUTS OF AMERICA
And RIDGE RD the MONMOUTH JUNCTION KINGSTON home KILGORE
    CENTER of DOW JONES & CO. INC. the ACCESS CARD REQUIRED brave
    STOP FOR PEDESTRIAN IN CROSSWALK

★

O magic property say the stunning can people perform you break and see
    the svelte
By George tobacco the organized reunion dawn's masquerade
    hospitalization early and late light buys time
What insinuation instinct so phony baloney proudly all ears we pierced
    earrings hailed in Germany
At peanut gallery the easy chair twilight's batty procession last chocolate
    milkshake gleaming metal teeth

Whose underwear beat broad instrumental choices stripes breakfast together
    and Mephistopheles paused bright *eminence grise* stars daily ormolu
Through insincere penises the pleasant song perilous to stand fight flavor city
O'er stomach disease the body snatchers ramparts blocked life we pissed
    away watched houses soused
Were milked through so promised margins gallantly breathing double
    streaming blood sauce

And monumental feathers the purple pastime rocket's smashed windows
    red desk sauce glare and crayon
The piecemeal ceegar bombs broken homes bursting in sun in tooth holes
    air patrol verst
Gave strong rinsing proof of falsehood through bony shorts the presser
    fessed night blessed seconds
That amnesia bled our bitchy stable flag stiff stupefying was meat potatoes
    still family fate there on ice

O manic prosperity say pick off does chop suey that hat hook star on
    nightly spangled kid stuff banner basket case yet maintain position
    wave at Mommy
O'er Hamburger Heaven the bone takes land down yonder of polished
    holsters the baseball darkness free talk cure
And previous inhabitants the perverse response home candy pacification of
    washing machines the broken pipe brave brown face

★

for Jackson Mac Low (1922–2004)

O Elvis say Samizdat can Leavenworth you Allah see poltroon
By Frankenstein the Virgin dawn's Roger early tutu light Remington
What Haman so Plain of Jars proudly fama we Horace hailed Samuel
At Peter and Paul the Sausalito twilight's Lima last Ramadan gleaming lambda

Whose Oswald broad Oz stripes Popeye and Everglades bright Sanhedrin stars
    Miles Davis
Through McDonald's the Lhasa perilous Saracen fight burgermeisters
O'er Plutonic the Magoo ramparts Saigon we pleasaunce watched Samson
Were Pygmy so Hottentot gallantly Lou Gehrig streaming harmonielehre

And Jesus the Prometheus rocket's marchioness red Rasputin glare
    Rostropovich
The Trocadero bombs Oregon bursting Sumeria in Reich air Oppenheimer
Gave Tories proof Surinam through mauvaise foi the Albigensian night
    Jansenist
That Iphegenia our Baltic flag Cisalpine was Lacedemonian still Bessarabian
    there Santander

O Rome say Mauritania does Lusitania that Cuba star Rotterdam spangled
    Bastille banner Transylvania yet Transnistria wave Soyuz
O'er Saul and Paul the hootenanny land Doomsday of Rorschach the Greco-
    Roman free origami
And Plantagenet the schmuck home mestizo of ne'erdowell the Wonderland
    brave sirrah

Places in Dreams

O Flatbush Ave. say an old hotel in the jungle can outside a boutique you far
   below see a bridge over a river
By the Jersey City shoreline the house on a hillside dawn's ethnographic
   museum early English girls' school light in the 1920s
What on the subway so a friend's parents' suburban house proudly a walled
   town in the north we an island bird sanctuary hailed a palatial hall
At a suburban train station the big ships in a river out the window twilight's
   amusement park last rural Florida gleaming Nevada

Whose under a wedding tent broad a cottage stripes a Japanese restaurant in
   New York and raised reservoir bright small Catholic city stars a hotel set into a
   hillside
Through my old high school the coffeeshop perilous bus station in Pittsburgh
   fight bus to Chicago
O'er a bus through old suburbs the in the Midwest ramparts Middleburg,
   Virginia we New Jersey watched a riverbank
Were an island so cobwebbed steps to the basement gallantly a path through
   woods streaming across fields

And a restaurant the South Orange rocket's building with retail on the ground
   floor red Montrose Ave. glare the beach
The Uncle Milton's office bombs a park bench bursting Montrose Ave. in a
   dock with a powerboat air Warsaw's Jewish section
Gave Vienna's Jewish section proof a restaurant through a church the flat
   gray landscape night Siracusa
That Prague's unappealing palace our health food store flag Nova Scotia was
   suburban library still Camp Kennebec Junior dining hall there a city street

O Harvard Square say a Jewish shop does a comfortable living room that
busstop lit by streetlamps star south of Lincoln Center spangled New
Jersey banner 168th St. in Manhattan yet iron railroad bridge wave
near Columbia
O'er Vermont the house in Maplewood land Eastern Europe in 1848 of high-
school prom the Bosnia free gloomy apartment
And Camp Kennebec Senior the trash pit in the woods home an old house
of Avenue X the villa outside Budapest brave parking lots in Rome

★

O lockerrooms say mortgages can Billy you nine see handkerchiefs
By lassoes the messages dawn's bathhouse early potions light bombshelters
What method so magazine proudly crows we angels hailed blue
At oracles the explanatory twilight's robe last gun gleaming oil

Whose boat broad horoscope stripes psychs and boils bright polish stars
    pain
Through Michael the bandit perilous eggs fight grime
O'er lamplight the mark ramparts beginning we tempered watched
    progress
Were crows so moreover gallantly salient streaming mortgages

And flowers the flowers rocket's pacemaker red bagels glare Pointillist
The minefield bombs tookame bursting payments in negative air factors
Gave songs proof buses through course the eminent night beef
That striking our doyenne flag racehorse was improper still toilet
    there hymen

O omnibus say danger does ammonia that boing star amnesia spangled
    banger banner mews yet Zemlinsky wave warlock
O'er palookas the mortgages land homeruns of ointments the boyhood free
    beavers
And distinguish the bulletproof home prospect of love the punchdrunk
    brave bebop

★

O irresponsible say frogs can north you blow see measly
By George the marker dawn's bandanna early flushing light breaks
What portion so davening proudly plush we moaked hailed eleven
At orifices the premium twilight's hush last cigarette gleaming semen

Whose bargain broad beaver stripes signs and persecutes bright fivers stars
    flivver
Through foolish the vampire perilous handkerchief fight smack
O'er poopoo the hairdo ramparts tapped we sealy watched humanity
Were eagles so dreadful gallantly emasculated streaming semen

And Moses the people rocket's hierarchy red fean glare back
The regular bombs succulent bursting tomatoes in myopia air control
Gave dreck proof pejorative through holes the president night train
That racist our noses flag brains was precious still imperfect there dead

O necks say paper does Tokyo that hinterland star done spangled dicks
    banner egg yet soulful wave bye
O'er pizza the meaning land done of forceful the nail free bark
And plain the bat home glory of open the boys brave imagination

From a Red 2003 Standard Diary

O Friday July 4 say (during our fraudulent war) can I awakened to a sunny
    morning. you I wish we had see a whole week
By in Columbia County. the Charlotte's right eye is dawn's almost completely
    closed. Early Liz called and said light they had a total rainout
What in East Hampton yesterday, so and it's very wet proudly and cloudy
    this morning. we A good thing hailed we came up here.
At Louisa said Kitty's the probably gonna leave twilight's to get away from
    last bad memories of Martin. gleaming But maybe Kitty's sister

Whose will take the place. broad The allergy pill has stripes an odd
    calming effect. and It glues me bright to the green bench stars under
    the silver maple.
Through Then I walk up the road the in the heat perilous to Lipman's
    fields, fight just mowed,
O'er which I walk around the and observe. ramparts Then I water forsythia
    we and "stickerbushes" watched by the spring,
Were working up a sweat. so Then we all swim gallantly in the pond
    streaming for the first time

And this year. Not bad. the I got a terrific bee sting rocket's leaving the
    water. red Louisa weedwhacked glare the shady area.
The During lunch bombs under the silver maple, bursting Louisa told the
    girlies in the history air of her love life
Gave (a la Betty Smith). proof I told about through asking Owen's
    permission. the It took an hour night to drive to Josh
That and Dee's house our in Sharon, Connecticut. flag The girlies caught
    bullfrogs. was I proved to Peter, still Philip's brother-in-law, there I'm
    a good tennis player.

O Beth and her kids say were up at the house. does Louisa left us that by
the pond. star There was no food spangled and no bottle opener banner
for beer down there, yet so I wanted to go wave up to the house.
O'er At the house, the I mostly talked land to Philip or Beth of in the end.
the The fireworks were even better free than last time.
And The moon was the a yellow spike home on our drive home. of Back in
Gallatin, the Louisa and I watched brave fireflies in the field.

★

O vehicle say no can America you transgressing see guilt
By Iraq the occupation dawn's unknown early vessel light words
What holds so shapes proudly suffering we fraudulent hailed favorites
At form the days twilight's known last Americans gleaming expiation

Whose killing broad transports stripes my and our bright years stars
　　invasion
Through sights the guilt perilous days fight years
O'er form the Americans ramparts favorites we no watched Iraq
Were expiation so suffering gallantly my streaming transports

And fraudulent the invasion rocket's shapes red words glare transgressing
The vehicle bombs America bursting killing in vessel air holds
Gave unknown proof our through occupation the sights night guilt
That vehicle our shapes flag invasion was form still Iraq there Americans

O my say transgressing does sights that killing star years spangled vessel
　　banner our yet holds wave unknown
O'er no the America land transports of fraudulent the occupation free known
And words the my home known of expiation the days brave suffering

★

O monkey say design can sleep you price see meat
By loyalty the teeming dawn's tobacco early reason light sores
What denim so negligible proudly stains we seethe hailed legend
At music the young twilight's sedge last omen gleaming teacup

Whose bike broad dung stripes raiment and informs bright icicles
    stars same
Through signs the placement perilous eggs fight markers
O'er muscles the virtue ramparts bark we eggshells watched head
Were pierced so immune gallantly rod streaming disease

And without the pitched rocket's dime red dogs glare allies
The twofold bombs lack bursting highlights in Friday air portion
Gave home proof devastating through eager the song night tires
That inside our drudgery flag alive was snorkel still seedy there almond

O danger say elegant does temperance that demon star sham spangled lark
    banner insightful yet teased wave soul
O'er dark the sensational land deficit of olives the migrant free heat
And urns the stricture home tonic of text the leg brave aim

1957–2037

O 1957 say 1958 can 2034 you 1974 see 2029
By 1987 the 2014 dawn's 1994 early 2036 light 2019
What 2017 so 1968 proudly 1995 we 1964 hailed 2027
At 2015 the 1993 twilight's 1965 last 2023 gleaming 1959

Whose 2018 broad 1976 stripes 1997 and 2002 bright 1991 stars 1982
Through 1988 the 2005 perilous 1977 fight 2035
O'er 2007 the 1966 ramparts 2000 we 2003 watched 1971
Were 1983 so 2001 gallantly 1984 streaming 2010

And 1998 the 2016 rocket's 1972 red 1986 glare 2008
The 2013 bombs 1967 bursting 1963 in 2026 air 2022
Gave 1999 proof 2009 through 2028 the 1979 night 2020
That 1962 our 2032 flag 1961 was 1981 still 1992 there 1980

O 2012 say 1969 does 1996 that 1975 star 2031 spangled 2004 banner 1960
    yet 2006 wave 1973
O'er 2024 the 2033 land 1990 of 2021 the 1970 free 1989
And 1985 the 2025 home 1978 of 2030 the 2011 brave 2037

A Few of My Favorite Things

for John Coltrane

O cinnamon say wildflowers can candles you overheard conversations see
    the hottest day
By night heatbugs the small islands dawn's cottage cheese early basketball
    light sunsets
What pistachios so train rides proudly steamer clams we clouds hailed snow
At fried calimari the fireflies twilight's cross-country skiing last steeples
    gleaming fatty bacon

Whose sliver moon broad first light stripes foghorns and strawberry
    shortcake bright misty nights stars almonds
Through photos of dead relatives the sugar perilous Randall's Island
    asylum fight rocky coasts
O'er barbecue ribs the European novels ramparts gasoline smell we white
    stones watched coffee
Were horseradish so car radio gallantly ship horns in New York Harbor
    streaming incense

And peanut butter the wind rocket's sea glass red Swiss cheese glare seltzer
The yellow roses bombs country music bursting prime rib in sweet potatoes
    air berry bushes
Gave sweat stains proof foie gras through rum and Coke the soft vanilla ice
    cream night Latin literature
That audio books our green apples flag tomato juice was mint tea still
    country drives there weed

O cold swims say balsam pillows does cream soda that American poetry
    star Free Jazz spangled Prospect Park banner baths yet obituaries wave
    Belgian beer
O'er rare roast beef the cashews land black beans of audio recorders the
    '60s oldies free miles of mudflats
And blue cheese the oysters home blackberry jam of birdcalls the turnips
    brave cigarettes

★

O compulsive say words can plastic you positive see force
By torque the sand dawn's omniscience early allegations light decision
What pent so falsify proudly lake we forked hailed happenings
At family the taste twilight's elephants last fraught gleaming soupy

Whose behoove broad outside stripes cigar and opera bright letter
    stars heavens
Through erase the faucets perilous Tabasco fight mathematical
O'er rascal the lasting ramparts mace we laughter watched Oregon
Were eleven so septic gallantly marked streaming stripes

And nostrum the open rocket's flies red holsters glare lozenge
The ducts bombs lice bursting lances in cells air superior
Gave ants proof aftermaths through flavors the doves night slime
That master our freights flag teeth was apples still level there harpoon

O somatic say pontoon does sauce that tupelo star absence spangled
    disease banner roster yet investigations wave leather
O'er talcum the lathers land onions of lapidary the sooth free fume
And tokens the embraces home green of slake the implant brave fish

★

O houses say flames can safe you superior see holy
By applications the heart dawn's races early teeth light horses
What apples so sauce proudly allowance we appropriate hailed slice
At hurt the brace twilight's soft last rice gleaming queen

Whose sandwiches broad blue stripes gas and basketballs bright disease
    stars rake
Through green the token perilous open fight lake
O'er freights the taste ramparts fasten we falsify watched implant
Were lasting so sand gallantly behoove streaming leg

And opera the gray rocket's lances red origin glare cells
The absence bombs doves bursting embraces in parkas air flakes
Gave offices proof soap through locket the tamp night sins
That frank our slime flag pork was aced still assassin there plenty

O eleven say decision does heavens that outside star level spangled erase
    banner letter yet holsters wave master
O'er south the logs land operation of positive the sausage free roster
And forked the orifice home lozenge of ducts the omniscience brave leather

Visions

O close your eyes say silver stalks grow out of the black earth can a silver
    tree soars down you if we become yellow see if we become a small silver
    wheel turning
By a purple pyramid dissolves in the orange the pair of black specks falling
    dawn's a monoplane at an airfield early a white pyramid of light light
    white plants grow tall
What a puff of white smoke above a house so three yellow candles proudly
    yellow tentacles we a golden rain falls during the night hailed fat
    bubbles of mercury float up
At a huge black cow the yellow river flows across the black earth twilight's
    a black queen sits on a golden throne last do people and cats turn white
    when electrocuted gleaming God drinks this orangeade

Whose orange ladder descends into our hearts broad a musical note floats
    upward in the orange stripes the balloons float up and up and glowing
    white fish swim through the darkness bright black dots bounce away in
    every direction stars two black dots cling to each other
Through a purple turtle the tiny sun being born, shining, blowing up
    perilous two silver rivers flow together fight the silver sun, with delicate
    threadlike rays
O'er a star drowning in the black water the white seat made from
    spiderwebs ramparts black butterflies with lime outlines we brown
    mold eats away the torso watched a profile tries to emerge
Were a turquoise vase so a pulsing candlestick gallantly a big yellow hole
    in the middle streaming we see the surface of the sun

And silver hair spreads out in the water the shoots come out of a tree
    stump rocket's this blue being, this purple being, flies around the
    landscape red each constellation a different insect glare the gold
    letters are unreadable
The turn into golden mist bombs light is. Light isn't. Light is bursting the
    world is not beginning in it leads into the past air before the raccoon face

Gave a yellow translucent fish, a ghost fish, feeding proof the surface of the
    world is tree bark through a bear's head, a werewolf's head, a cat's head
    the gold letter H night a white mountaineer
That a tunnel of overarching trees our beings, cracked beings, reflected in
    water flag worlds never quite born was bits of curdled milk in the black
    liquid of the world still a young white oak, reaching out to me with
    many arms there living under a giant jellyfish

O a big blue bat, a big blue bird say a raspberry sun behind a black mountain
    does a large yellow N tilts to the right that light leaks into the bottom of
    the world star the eye bounces between bright flames and dark shadows
    spangled there's a golden clash of civilizations banner an orange tree
    pulses yet a crucifixion wave a plane's wing bursts into flames
O'er a galleon, reflected in the river the frightened animal's open mouth
    land a table covered with candles of a large hole at the top of the world
    the cars drive toward me with muffled headlights free an animal sitting
    high in a tree
And wearing an archbishop's hat the tadpole's face, with eyes and mouth of
    light home the grassblades are made of light of the spiderwebs are made
    of light the woman's head turns into a horse's head brave her hands seem
    to be in flames

★

O boymel say ortons can samangra you floob see soob
By soinga the melid dawn's fabber early slava light dangla
What zemma so pletid proudly zangala we tangered hailed linedry
At slemmer the neggid twilight's byelin last vlagra gleaming seadoe

Whose elid broad sedent stripes limeba and devons bright semegra stars
    fombom
Through dollid the oilent perilous delson fight simeing
O'er telsiai the limmick ramparts dinade we sulled watched plibra
Were pressied so hemisful gallantly deselled streaming sebroth

And sumid the legga rocket's temid red petha glare danegray
The bremid bombs selvon bursting hoyster in dembotic air chaiding
Gave braister proof memid through sylligic the bornity night tongra
That syllibius our squillid flag soliast was soddized still selid there snedra

O beeyou say myla does wella that soiming star holing spangled curid
    banner dousa yet hemid wave anglo
O'er prevous the hollid land smander of bensus the sonid free seedbo
And degger the helgot home sandrac of dunpul the doypy brave boysun

★

O Indo-European say sister can eat you come see door
By yoke the brother dawn's beech early gall light juice
What mill so thrush proudly sweet we wasp hailed west
At bond the weave twilight's daughter last sew gleaming mother

Whose cerebrum broad snow stripes cow and sit bright burgher stars lie
Through nit the new perilous sacred fight name
O'er tame the penis ramparts ford we potion watched wear
Were wed so stand gallantly bear streaming mouse

And ass the winter rocket's chin red sing glare eagle
The light bombs beaver bursting fear in meat air wild
Gave louse proof mind through young the moon night swine
That mead our bee flag summer was goat still beget there grace

O spleen say quick does tree that starling star justice spangled brow
     banner lox yet tongue wave night
O'er swallow the apple land lip of star the birch free oars
And credo the thin home slough of guest the go brave day

The Triumph of the Red States in 2004

O Ohio say Wisconsin can Idaho you Georgia see Texas
By North Carolina the Tennessee dawn's Vermont early Oklahoma light
    California
What Maine so Washington proudly Colorado we South Dakota hailed Illinois
At New Mexico the Connecticut twilight's Indiana last Maryland gleaming
    Oregon

Whose Alabama broad Missouri stripes Arkansas and Kansas bright Delaware
    stars North Dakota
Through New Jersey the Montana perilous Hawaii fight Arizona
O'er South Carolina the Nevada ramparts West Virginia we Nebraska watched
    New York
Were Iowa so Alaska gallantly Mississippi streaming New Hampshire

And Utah the Virginia rocket's Wyoming red Pennsylvania glare Minnesota
The Michigan bombs Massachusetts bursting Kentucky in Rhode Island air
    Louisiana
Gave Florida proof North Carolina through Arkansas the Colorado night
    Alaska
That Nebraska our Oklahoma flag Utah was Iowa still Ohio there North
    Dakota

O Missouri say Alabama does Indiana that Idaho star New Mexico spangled
    Wyoming banner Virginia yet West Virginia wave Georgia
O'er South Carolina the Texas land South Dakota of Mississippi the Arizona
    free Montana
And Kentucky the Kansas home Nevada of Tennessee the Louisiana brave
    Florida

★

O Momaday say pitterpatter can legacies you squirrel see rostrums
By mace the précis dawn's platitude early softening light Turkey
What pregnancy so dollopy proudly positioned we premium hailed police
At manufacturing the boisterous twilight's pawns last moins gleaming
    Gleason

Whose meg broad tire stripes pomegranate and doilies bright Simon
    stars ploys
Through monuments the placid perilous celestial fight piano
Oe'r toilets the basketball ramparts tangle we eagles watched deliverance
Were irascible so mellifluent gallantly processed streaming peacepipes

And melanin the boreal rocket's tiedye red pressure glare anvil
The beggary bombs satisfaction bursting elegance in pelican air selfhood
Gave April proof ransom through rundowns the pellicle night breast
That ambulance our saucer flag cheapskate was treading still awesome
    there kazoo

O harmonica say braindead does Malcolm that passive star cluttered
    spangled background banner antlers yet demonstrable wave semblances
O'er Pegasus the pleasurable land found of Evelyn the damaging free reese
And biblical the typography home magnetic of steam the lease brave mailman

★

O Borodin say arrangements can forthright you infant see piecemeal
By cinema the implacable dawn's toys early morganatic light sigh
What pukey so relish proudly orgiastic we settees hailed mire
At dominant the fibbed twilight's oaks last runcible gleaming tea

Whose regime broad gold stripes bazaar and angry bright Sioux stars
    horseradish
Through stain the apple perilous panties fight alligator
O'er clock the restless ramparts seizure we angular watched popsicle
Were demonstrations so masked gallantly gophers streaming magazine

And yogurt the dressing rocket's colors red minus glare naked
The flakes bombs metal bursting worker in diamond air mine
Gave peeling proof mortgage through savings the diamond night sex
That tangential our emerald flag marmoreal was stupor still virgin
    there teeth

O placeholders say ruby does soybean that jars star moiety spangled
    lackadaisical banner elephant yet trains wave engine
O'er dirt the mescal land sauce of longwinded the sapphire free finger
And raft the deranged home wait of bank the suit brave handles

Times to Come

O sealed borders say flood damage can brain drain you DNA tests see rich kids
By designer drugs the extreme sports dawn's mold early overspending light
    overeating
What bloated military so strongmen proudly quiet euthanasias we servants hailed
    investment advisers
At benefit cuts the angry talk shows twilight's country estates last caretakers
    gleaming cellphone towers

Whose earphones broad video screens stripes cleaning crews and home attendants
    bright sales associates stars the destitute
Through doubling up the suicides perilous metal detectors fight bomb-sniffing dogs
O'er DNA tests the technological collapse ramparts mold we earphones watched
    new weather
Were infomercials so gated communities gallantly angry talk shows streaming
    drug-resistant bacteria

And financial scandals the underground economy rocket's Hobbesian continents
    red tax havens glare sealed borders
The water shortages bombs video screens bursting crumbling infrastructure in
    gridlock air consultants
Gave fundamentalism proof decadence through suicides the brain drain night
    foundations
That overspending our discounters flag the destitute was prisons still overeating
    there sex tourists

O emergency rooms say tripling up does begging that party planners star creative
    outpouring spangled Alzheimer's banner new weather and flora yet light shows
    wave quiet euthanasias
O'er faded tattoos the benefit cuts land sycophancy of front men the realists free
    cellphone towers
And metal detectors the mechanical breakdowns home closed-off regions of organs
    for sale the addictions brave talk of end times

America's Overseas Military Bases

O Camp Fallujah say Forward Operating Base Abu Ghraib can Combat
    Outpost Shocker you Joint Base Balad see Victory Base Complex
By Camp Bucca the Camp Justice dawn's Camp Taji early Forward
    Operating Base Grizzly light Forward Operating Base Sykes
What Camp Baharia so Bagram Air Base proudly Camp Dwyer we Camp
    Leatherneck hailed Forward Operating Base Delaram
At Shindand Air Base the Kandahar International Airport twilight's NATO
    Support Activity Belgium last Chievres Air Base gleaming Diego Garcia
    Navy Support Facility

Whose Ansback broad Bamberg stripes Baumholder and Darmstadt bright
    Giessen Depot/Ray Barracks stars Geilenkirchen Air Base
Through Giebelstadt the Grafenwoehr perilous Hanau fight Heidelberg
O'er Hohenfels the Illesheim ramparts Kaiserlautern we Kitzingen watched
    Mannheim
Were Ramstein Air Base so Rhein-Main Air Base gallantly Schweinfurt Air
    Base streaming Spangdahlem Air Base

And Stuttgart/Robinson Barracks the Vilseck rocket's Wiesbaden red
    Wuerzburg glare Souda Bay Naval Support Activity
The Thule Air Base bombs Keflaavik Naval Air Station bursting Aviano Air
    Base in Camp Darby air Caserma Ederle
Gave Gaeta Naval Support Activity proof La Maddalena Naval Support
    Activity through Naples Naval Support Activity the Sigonella Naval Air
    Station night Atsugi Naval Air Facility
That Camp S.D. Butler our Camp Zama flag Iwakuni Marine Corps Air
    Station was Kadena Air Base still Misawa Air Base there Sasebo
    Fleet Activities

O Torii Station say Yokosuka Fleet Activities does Yokota Air Base that 254th
    Base Support Battalion star Lajes Field spangled Logistics Group Western
    Pacific banner Camp Casey yet Camp Henry wave Camp Hialeah
O'er Camp Humphreys the Kunsan Air Base land Osan Air Base of Moron
    Air Base the Rota Naval Station free Incirlik
And Izmir Air Station the Joint Military Facility St. Mawgan home
    Lakenheath RAF of Mildenhall RAF the Molesworth RAF brave
    Guantanamo Bay Naval Station

★

O Tory propensities say awesome salamander can artificial toystores you
    mortgage petunias see pregnant escarole
By Dalmatians joining the narcotic soma dawn's pretzel relief early
    ammunition tape light lissome target
What delegations trove so olive dimestores proudly dutiful porkchops we
    nailed fires hailed orotund sheens
At omnibus refrigeration the dollop sister twilight's icicle silverware last
    Mohawk Power gleaming seagull soup

Whose oratorical soupspoon broad elementary patter stripes pastry humbug
    and pellicle Egremont bright dandelion salvation stars chuck insensible
Through minute timecakes the selfsame eggshell perilous Army Navy fight
    soluble boil
Oe'r regulated eating the processed pondlife ramparts template memorial we
    eminent donut watched toolchests exhale
Were primetime fogies so elevated infrastructure gallantly boisterous Hellgate
    streaming deed exhaustion

And oracular mesquite the prognosis times rocket's Telemann redwing red
    develop led glare soiled Einhoven
The noisy tangram bombs loyal coinage bursting to-go pantsuit in parked
    Loyola's air chromatic passenger
Gave poignant dartboard proof tuliptree omnibus through seminal pretzel the
    masked elevator night oil timeshare
That pugnacious restart our felt banana flag laughing potatoes was beat
    brown still inky oil there belting registrations

O placename dilapidate say mandibles talcum does racewar space that
    bamboozled toreador star registered messenger spangled rather
    parturition banner timid Titleist yet eagerly defense wave hoisted tar
O'er particular raindates the magnetic earlybird land tostados origin of
    tapeworm spaghetti the melted testimonial free beeswax solvent
And progressive telecommunication the mismatched peel home parson
    rural of majority teahouse the levelheaded decibel brave soldered
    appointment

★

O oildrops say hospitality can noises you exchange see pondwillows
By roads the hold dawn's donut early miscalculation light oars
What elephantine so stolid proudly ingratiating we hyena hailed celltowers
At individual the manual twilight's brogan last porcupine gleaming
　　meatsauce

Whose armrest broad illicit stripes dominate and infinity bright engineered
　　stars plunge
Through marquees the almond perilous fruitcake fight tangle
O'er music the safety ramparts breeze we easement watched rockdove
Were rope so indicative gallantly homogenized streaming eggnog

And purified the rock rocket's birth red trap glare infantile
The ambrosial bombs promise bursting frogeggs in diversions air alibi
Gave sonorous proof blood through holdups the arrangement night keyhole
That orioles our bottle flag stolen was limping still droplets there vacant

O boysroom say love does inner that ostrich star signal spangled borax
　　banner tearstained yet tonsils wave beyond
O'er grandma the envelope land rippling of eastern the memory free
　　wrapper
And behind the catch home slowdown of timely the oatmeal brave horror

House Republican Leaders Violating
the Ten Commandments

O Dennis Hastert worship other gods say Tom DeLay name the Lord in vain
can Roy Blunt desecrate the Sabbath you Richard Pombo dishonor thy
parents see Joe Barton kill
By Thomas Davis commit adultery the Doc Hastings steal dawn's Thomas
Reynolds bear false witness early Bob Ney covet light Peter Hoekstra steal
What Bob Goodlatte worship other gods so Henry Hyde desecrate the Sabbath
proudly William Thomas name the Lord in vain we John Shadegg dishonor
thy parents hailed Donald Manzullo commit adultery
At Don Young bear false witness the Steve Buyer kill twilight's Christopher
Cox covet last David Dreier name the Lord in vain gleaming Jim Nussle
steal

Whose John Boehner covet broad Jerry Lewis dishonor thy parents stripes
Duncan Hunter desecrate the Sabbath and F. James Sensenbrenner
commit adultery bright Deborah Pryce bear false witness stars Michael
Oxley kill
Through Sherwood Boehlert worship other gods the Bob Ney name the Lord
in vain perilous William Thomas bear false witness fight Steve Buyer
desecrate the Sabbath
O'er Henry Hyde steal the Donald Manzullo kill ramparts Sherwood Boehlert
worship other gods we Roy Blunt commit adultery watched Don Young
dishonor thy parents
Were Jim Nussle covet so John Shadegg steal gallantly Thomas Reynolds
commit adultery streaming Doc Hastings name the Lord in vain

And John Boehner covet the Thomas Davis kill rocket's Deborah Pryce
dishonor thy parents red Duncan Hunter desecrate the Sabbath glare Peter
Hoekstra worship other gods
The Michael Oxley bear false witness bombs F. James Sensenbrenner steal
bursting Christopher Cox commit adultery in Bob Goodlatte dishonor thy
parents air Tom DeLay bear false witness

Gave Dennis Hastert desecrate the Sabbath proof David Dreier covet
through Jerry Lewis name the Lord in vain the Joe Barton worship
other gods night Richard Pombo kill
That Jim Nussle worship other gods our Bob Ney name the Lord in vain
flag Steve Buyer desecrate the Sabbath was Christopher Cox kill
still Deborah Pryce steal there F. James Sensenbrenner dishonor thy
parents

O Thomas Davis covet say Duncan Hunter bear false witness does Richard
Pombo commit adultery that Henry Hyde steal star Michael Oxley bear
false witness spangled Sherwood Boehlert dishonor thy parents banner
David Dreier worship other gods yet Jerry Lewis name the Lord in vain
wave Donald Manzullo covet
O'er Joe Barton kill the John Boehner commit adultery land Don Young
desecrate the Sabbath of Peter Hoekstra dishonor thy parents the
William Thomas commit adultery free Bob Goodlatte desecrate the
Sabbath
And Thomas Reynolds worship other gods the Doc Hastings steal home
John Shadegg covet of Roy Blunt bear false witness the Tom DeLay kill
brave Dennis Hastert name the Lord in vain

★

O bring dogs say the sooth can elegant headdress you pulsate wildly see practice
    regions
By pellicle nights the marked minefield dawn's operatic hawsers early
    evangelical downs light polite pines
What relevant elephant so bright finds proudly raining catsup we Episcopal
    sights hailed necessary Orcs
At bland platoons the noisome fridge twilight's bred bargain last people like
    gleaming magazine birds

Whose invented session broad reading foray stripes sandy reezes and apparent
    rationing bright force oval stars legendary health
Through brackish polls the exaggerated price perilous digging sites fight
    homing religion
O'er primary milestones the apron basket ramparts soften lime we eel leap
    watched pregnant ranges
Were rancid argyle so imaginary eyes gallantly breathing yolk streaming ready Andes

And precise membrane the boiling ointment rocket's beaver ordinance red
    melting hologram glare breast divulged
The poison eggs bombs highway minimums bursting leg bites in soda finery air
    icing tooth
Gave suspect grace proof immediate rice through polish living the mindless
    seesaw night raspberry felt
That rescheduled oak our purebred cart flag racing moth was bent severally
    still perpetrator deluxe there ransomed rind

O bridging ring say ominous harmony does recent feelgood that practiced
    merchandise star original dimming spangled donnybrook purity banner
    delegate peace yet brimming parsecs wave holistic resins
O'er yellow saints the melded press land parted redder of pagan development
    the blest negligee free eagle eye
And purified horn the vegetative fife home filling plastic of painted eyesight
    the burning tools brave unsecured pottage

★

O smiling say primetime can icecream you holiday see mandragons
By Jesus the sweaty dawn's holistic early messages light Bradley
What Oliver so oracular proudly hospital we easystreet hailed amplifiers
At Easter the whirligig twilight's Europe last peacepipe gleaming racquets

Whose eggs broad diesel stripes lakefront and silvered bright parking
    stars monument
Through breasts the baseball perilous order fight policyholder
O'er pelvic the slap ramparts cushioning we raindate watched obsessively
Were impregnable so estimable gallantly ricecrispies streaming steak

And braggadocio the piney rocket's dogsock red delegation glare polymer
The politic bombs evaluating bursting sagacious in mineshaft air pregnancy
Gave coffee proof illegitimate through bildungsroman the blastingcaps
    night umbrella
That Rapallo our rhyming flag boysenberry was anointed still plastic
    there filing

O broad say frames does dressing that earlybird star lined spangled
    dollhouse banner pause yet belvedere wave diagnosis
O'er miles the breakneck land pearly of militant the crowds free Heisenberg
And raindate the pirates home elevation of together the oyster brave belt

The Elimination of the U.S. Soccer Team at the 2006 World Cup

O U.S. on counterattack say the right time can a man down you knock him
down see the most expensive player
By trailing at the half the little slip here dawn's straddling the line of
bankruptcy early he never broke light gives it up
What not going in the right direction so their fair share proudly dangerous
play we clear it hailed great looks
At any other ball the stand up twilight's round of 16 last to take the free
kick gleaming corrals this one

Whose restart here broad trying to get the inside position stripes his
United States jersey and always right on the verge bright on the top of
strikers stars Ghana's gonna milk this
Through rumble of electricity the here in Nuremburg perilous the United
States in a must win fight everywhere he goes
O'er Juventus in Italy the right into the post ramparts inside the box we in
the 67th minute watched golden opportunity
Were really working hard so how fit the U.S. team is gallantly back over to
the U.S.A. streaming will fitness

And the U.S.A. in full attack mode the exactly what the U.S.A. wanted
rocket's offside once more for the United States red shot of Times
Square glare a tie does nothing
The go against the United States bombs presented by Adidas bursting his
service down the wing in spark on the outside air the last substitute
Gave foul against the U.S.A. proof time beginning to be a factor through no
foul on this play the he made a bad call night a dentist by trade
That Germany is his home our man of the match flag another foul was not
many chances still as good as this one there not a strong effort

O drive it into the six-yard box say can the U.S. help itself does this
    booming kick that someone on a mad run star play the ball forward
    spangled with a free kick banner not enough yet couldn't get around
    wave losing it
O'er a man down the corner for the U.S.A. land the man down of wait on
    him the fitness free stitch in the side
And their fate on this day the four years of dreaming home on the verge of
    elimination of set pieces the that simple brave run out the rest of the time

★

O stone say horse can song you time see run
By safe the leg dawn's ape early soft light tank
What ice so pike proudly cap we tag hailed lock
At mop the pop twilight's home last tongs gleaming ox

Whose sake broad brace stripes table and nape bright broil stars voice
Through hurt the pencil perilous breech fight ice
O'er eagle the season ramparts mail we hoard watched solid
Were top so more gallantly taste streaming hung

And ping the toll rocket's oak red snow glare news
The alike bombs time bursting bike in halt air boil
Gave hoist proof omen through orange the poor night dog
That log our way flag day was story still level there strange

O hay say toys does ply that island star base spangled aim banner oil yet
    play wave date
O'er borscht the brains land angels of park the bog free point
And mice the place home rake of time the breaks brave dock

★

O adventure say Almagest can anorectic you armor see automation
By baroque the berkelium dawn's blazon early Bowling Green light bulb
What camelopard so cataplasia proudly Cheapside we clamant hailed
    colostrums
At conscious the cotton twilight's cryostat last date line gleaming
    deoxygenate

Whose dip broad Domitian stripes Dzungaria and embellishment bright
    escape stars eye
Through fianchetto the fluorosis perilous French Polynesia fight gateway
    drug
O'er go the Groves ramparts Harpy we hide watched hour
Were image so infirmary gallantly ionization streaming jugular

And kreplach the leaves rocket's lithograph red Macbeth glare mark
The memorandum bombs Minneconjou bursting morphogenesis in
    Napoleon III air nitrohydrochloric acid
Gave occlude proof orgasm through painter the pataphysics night Persian
    Gulf
That pink our police flag preconceive was pronunciation still pyromancy
    there ration

O remainder say Richardson does rudderfish that Sao Vicente star sea bass
    spangled set banner sickle cell yet smack wave space sickness
O'er stakeholder the stratigraphy land Sun Yat-sen of tachymeter the
    tension free tilbury
And transference the tupelo home ungainly of varicocele the voice brave weird

A Few of My Favorite Things in American Poetry

(through the 1970s)

O Lyrics of a Lowly Life say The Lost World can Hugh Selwyn Mauberley
    you In Cold Hell, in Thicket see New Goose
By The Materials the Al Que Quiere dawn's Observations early Elegiac
    Feelings American light Words
What The Dream Songs so As We Know proudly Spoon River Anthology we
    Day by Day hailed Smoke and Steel
At Poeta en Nueva York the Kora in Hell twilight's Mexico City Blues last
    Democratic Vistas gleaming Stanzas in Meditation

Whose Spring and All broad Montage of a Dream Deferred stripes The
    Pisan Cantos and Stanzas for Iris Lezak bright The Children of the
    Night stars Ariel
Through Passport to Horror the Poems perilous 55 Poems fight &
O'er Lunar Baedecker the Mobile ramparts Memory we New Hampshire
    watched Black Riders
Were Rivers and Mountains so The Waste Land gallantly What Are Years?
    streaming Kaddish

And White Buildings the Sour Grapes rocket's The Cities red Battle Pieces
    glare For Love
The Saint Judas bombs Prufrock and Other Observations bursting Life
    Studies in The Bean Eaters air The Innocent Doves
Gave The Good European proof After Lorca through A Boy's Wish the
    Riprap night The Wedge
That Meditations in an Emergency our Leaves of Grass flag War Is Kind was
    The Raven and Other Poems still Harmonium there The Fire Screen

O The Double Dream of Spring say A does Poems by Emily Dickinson that
    On the Wing star Water Street spangled Three Poems banner Homage
    to Sextus Propertius yet The Far Field wave The Man With the Blue
    Guitar
O'er Tender Buttons the Summer Knowledge land Lunch Poems of The
    Sonnets the Reality Sandwiches free The Distances
And Studying Hunger Journals the Renascence home Howl of North &
    South the Clairvoyant Journal brave The Dead Lecturer

★

O oniongrass say slaw can cacophony you yulelog see statistics
By balustrades the theoretical dawn's doghouse early earwig light
    Lilliputian
What wagontrain so salivating proudly passive we weather hailed
    hopscotch
At aimless the thousand twilight's tastebud last lamppost gleaming gyro

Whose highlights broad babyfood stripes southern and allegorical bright
    billystick stars stallions
Through thimbles the timeframe perilous partypoopers fight nabobs
O'er ovary the tolerant ramparts razz we wilderness watched widebody
Were wholeheartedly so sarnographic gallantly gainsaid streaming
    signlanguage

And allotropic the telephone rocket's rasta red rapacious glare gogo
The tamed bombs bailiwick bursting bildungsromans in iodine air aperture
Gave geegaw proof Pomeranian through tapestry the tuberose night
    Nashville
That Theseus our oildrum flag faithless was wattles still saintly there
    tomahawk

O oliveoil say samurai does dunegrass that tiller star sincere spangled
    spaceship banner boomerang yet yesman wave welcome
O'er omens the tailings land Lazarus of owlglass the thalidomide free
    fumigation
And arrangements the tollbooth home humidifier of osteopath the townhall
    brave bilge

★

O petridish say olive can pants you roundabout see placemarks
By rightful the branch dawn's purposeful early bark light beginning
What birth so muscular proudly icing we organism hailed dodger
At responsible the ligament twilight's brogans last honor-roll
    gleaming origami

Whose yumyum broad orangejuice stripes person and magazine bright
    polish stars embark
Through mindgames the almond perilous monkey fight perforation
O'er lard the escalator ramparts possible we irrigate watched song
Were tether so aboveboard gallantly eggplant streaming rock

And itself the luff rocket's burdensome red oily glare cheese
The outstanding bombs plaques bursting designs in noon air hostess
Gave forgetful proof massive through peeling the mirth night rasp
That dumdum our pregnant flag basking was hurtled still egret
    there original

O hostel say swami does uncork that ransom star gurgling spangled
    raspberry banner undulate yet perform wave kindly
Oe'r denial the prescient land rising of essential the sight free bath
And welcome the lost home force of smoking the antsy brave buying

A Few of My Favorite Things in T.S. Eliot

O Rachel *née* Rabinovitch say the latest Pole can the thousand sordid
    images you in the juvescence of the year see the eternal Footman
By talking of Michelangelo the dead tree gives no shelter dawn's what
    might have been early the shaking of her breasts light bats with baby
    faces
What Shantih so in my beginning proudly the door we never opened we
    among velleities hailed never and always
At shored against my ruins the Gentile or Jew twilight's death had undone
    so many last aimless smile gleaming a Greek was murdered

Whose Sir Ferdinand Klein broad spawned in some estaminet in Antwerp
    stripes my buried life and female smells bright pearls that were his eyes
    stars there will be time
Through the future futureless the quick now, here perilous not knowing
    what to feel fight his laughter was submarine
O'er disturb the universe the neither living nor dead ramparts to prepare a
    face we infinitely suffering thing watched in demotic French
Were in the last desert so the lean solicitor gallantly a golden grin
    streaming a lusterless protrusive eye

And Chicago Semite Viennese the phthisic hand rocket's Unreal City red a
    thousand furnished rooms glare time for you
The hundred visions and revisions bombs an age of prudence bursting I am
    no prophet in I have lost my passion air that is not it
Gave an overwhelming question proof them pills I took through an old crab
    with barnacles the with a pained surprise night hope for the wrong thing
That in a rented house our the pain of living flag voices singing in our ears
    was the eternal enemy still there are no eyes here there the rats are
    underneath

O the Jew is underneath say with murderous paws does a crowd of
   twisted things that the tumid river star the beneficent spider spangled
   sempiternal though sodden banner the cruellest month yet the old
   miasmal mist wave HURRY UP PLEASE ITS TIME
O'er her friendly bust the polyphiloprogenitive land smell of steaks of
   memory and desire the Hieronymo's mad againe free if you came this way
And after such knowledge the I Tiresias home bowing among the Titians of
   each in his prison the Jew squats brave who clipped the lion's wings

★

O wretches say pine can nickels you teeth see briefs
By prize the negligence dawn's brocade early niceguys light eloquence
What breathalizer so slimy proudly masked we ate hailed leggings
At mailrooms the consequential twilight's baroque last refrigerating
    gleaming measles

Whose million broad sealskin stripes mastiffs and slakes bright puff
    stars slight
Through piers the elegant perilous priest fight natural
O'er slack the minute ramparts fork we accommodate watched faucet
Were peacemaking so noisy gallantly primetime streaming rice

And brief the rocky rocket's premise red felt glare prince
The suds bombs stacked bursting puke in nostrils air corpse
Gave pimps proof sandwich through tongue the breck night sour
That legend our bath flag integrity was palpable still bled there peerless

O Borodin say pace does meet that bellicose star breakfast spangled gym
    banner laster yet space wave drone
O'er potluck the pellet land regains of help the burgundy free feces
And regulate the salt home regency of pesticide the plebicite brave
    pistachios

★

O love say leeks can burn you pride see wardens
By pilot the informs dawn's soil early cream light brings
What doesn't so breakthrough proudly bastion we breathe hailed filigree
At brindled the procession twilight's dugout last alligator gleaming hearth

Whose bromide broad business stripes porcelain and images bright builder
    stars ancestor
Through even the sign language perilous poppy fight Newton
O'er melted the blessed ramparts eglantine we rhizome watched broom
Were ladled so bandaged gallantly sealed streaming freezer

And restaurateur the liaison rocket's booth red tangrams glare sensitive
The organ bombs worldling bursting pippin in drag air ermine
Gave balance proof Calvary through soup the reclining night noodle
That oblong our mouthpiece flag ammunition was violin still enticing
    there reason

O love say soften does worm that dysentery star reserve spangled felt
    banner markdown yet register wave almond
O'er reasonable the undigested land thigh of smell the respect free
    institution
And fading the peeking home invincible of brandishing the rug brave person

A Few of My Favorite Things in Allen Ginsberg

O Naomi Ginsberg say Eliot probably an ignu can masturbating in his jeep
    you the Flower burning in the Day see the penis of billionaires
By the same old universe the green leaf shaped like a human heart dawn's
    waiting at the wild edge early many a butterfly committed suicide light
    the Babylonian possible world
What Van Gogh's Ear on the currency so imbecilic canned voice of eternity
    proudly Denver! Denver! we'll return we hundreds of suitcases full of
    tragedy hailed in a minor universe
At death comes before life the driving drunk on boulevards twilight's
    every leaf has fallen before last money from an impossible saintly roll
    gleaming angelheaded hipsters

Whose Newark's bleak furnished room broad Greystone's foetid halls
    stripes time with all its falling leaves and fat women in strapless silk
    bright head & tail of the universe stars the old hotel of the world
Through archetype degenerate the radio screams for money perilous the
    skin trembles in happiness fight flying like birds into Time
O'er them bad Russians the actual visions & actual prisons ramparts
    dreamy strange murderer we what's *left over* from perfection watched
    fishqueen fugitive-com'd lapel
Were MY SECRET STORY ON TV so above the abandoned labyrinth gallantly
    yaketayakking screaming vomiting streaming World world world

And the universe is a graveyard the my bus will arrive as foretold rocket's
    sphinx of cement and aluminum red done with yourself at last glare
    ashen indoor eyes at hospitals
The all men fall bombs an archangelic cigarette bursting crude soul notes
    taken down in winter dusks of Brooklyn air naked in the dark, dreaming
Gave all night long until dawn proof Death, stay thy phantoms through
    unattainable desires the God sleeps! night Notable Frenchman of the Void
That Passaic and Ganges one our real as a dream flag purer than
    Greyhound was New York rotting still I send up my rocket there
    Playground of Phantoms

O Rotting Ginsberg say strychnine jizzum in his voice does a thousand
   lonely craps in gas stations that the madman is holy star Death let you
   out spangled lion that eats my mind banner what's left to dream, more
   Chinese meat? yet this cockroach is holy wave Neal, we'll be real heroes
   now
O'er Rilke at least could dream the vast lamb of the middleclass land in
   Bloomfield on a park bench of the sacred ruin of the world the huge cop
   by the Coke machine free all the governments will fall
And clover from Keats' grave the great faces worn down by rain home taste
   the shit of Being of Asia is rising against me the teeth made of white
   radios brave Roosevelt with gray eyeballs

★

O America say eats can dominate you retrogress see reason
By restant the demimondaine dawn's thwarts early muses light portends
What believes so impregnable proudly farted we forestall hailed ice cream
At vision the ascendant twilight's stands last mugs gleaming pisses

Whose bellows broad passion stripes handy and slaloms bright hazes
      stars lemma
Through bidet the tantamount perilous sieves fight sameday
O'er holster the songbird ramparts disease we pregnant watched oar
Were plugging so randazzle gallantly parks streaming visits

And responds the triumphant rocket's leather red fattens glare chills
The cellophane bombs forever bursting never in illustration air right-side
Gave slimy proof dildo through intones the miracle night reposes
That lasers our billygoat flag melt was irrelevant still begins there purple

O introject say finding does exonerate that needle star beeswax spangled
      informal banner Tintoretto yet broke wave releases
O'er blossom the smell land sizing of belief the breeze free momentarily
And hustles the fivesome home sprinkles of holidays the sodden
      brave America

★

O hope say finalizes can Bilbao you forever see lashes
By primary the duplicates dawn's ermine early tamps light springs
What bombards so exaggerates proudly understands we umbrellas
    hailed fustian
At dimbulb the immigration twilight's bend last Oregon gleaming eternal

Whose hope broad opening stripes jelly and artificial bright pulse
    stars dissembling
Through everything the plastic perilous forefends fight springs
O'er timepieces the impulse ramparts umbrage we toolchests watched play
Were underground so remnant gallantly mushrooms streaming eternal

And hope the impending rocket's Doppler red utterance glare funnels
The ransoms bombs electric bursting dee-dum in monumental air springs
Gave mutant proof ran through possibility the earnest night earlybird
That Posnan our organized flag restant was organ still developed
    there eternal

O hope say finalizes does portending that magnifies star often spangled
    deathrow banner opposite yet toilet wave doggone
O'er timepieces the impulse land mirage of destiny the pools free springs
And posits the foil home mine of embalmed the cure brave eternal

From a Red 2008 Standard Diary

O Tuesday November 4 Election Day (US) say Up at 8:40 after a deliciously
    long sleep, can just what I need for tonight, you working at the
    newspaper till 1:30 a.m. see After breakfast in the kitchen trashed
By by the twins and a sleepover friend, the I finally feel it, allow myself
    to feel it. dawn's Overwhelming joy. early Praise Jah! light I call Mom,
    Russ at the polls in Fla.,
What who warns me, "Beware of the evil eye." so I read Istvan Vas's great
    poem "The Grand Finale" proudly and burst into tears of joy and fury we
    at what we've lived with for 40 years, hailed almost my entire life.
At On the way to the polls with Louisa & Charlotte the at 10:40,
    I mortify Louisa. twilight's I tap Brooklyn Borough President last
    Marty Markowitz on the arm and say, "Praise God!"gleaming Marty
    Markowitz shrugs.

Whose "You are insane," Louisa says. broad Everyone's so nervous today.
    stripes They can't see what's happening, and the legacy of two close
    elections. bright Everyone's at John Jay H.S. stars Eric says the line's
    1½ hours long.
Through I can't wait that long. the Charlotte and I leave. perilous Eric
    catches us on the street. fight He offers me his place in the middle
    of line!
O'er That's still no good. the He suggests Charlotte stand in line for me.
    ramparts Louisa calls me from John Jay at 11:30. we I join her and
    Charlotte, and we wait until 12:25, watched bringing the total wait to
    one hour and 45 minutes.
Were What a fucking disgrace! so We wait with an older woman, some
    30-year-olds. gallantly Everyone looks blankly when I say streaming this
    is the most historic day in our lives.

And I'm the most boisterous person there. the The poll workers are partly
responsible for the wait, rocket's two lazy and inefficient women. red
Charlotte comes in the booth, pulls the levers for me. glare (Next time,
she can vote.)
The Walking out past the line, I whistle, bombs "Mine eyes have seen the
glory bursting of the coming of the Lord," in further embarrassing
Louisa. air I leave a half-hour late for work.
Gave On the subway, I hear it took a half-hour at P.S. 282. proof At the
Journal, no one knows anything concrete. through I call Russ again at
the polls. the He's worried the turnout is sparse. night I call Alice at the
DNC at 3,
That she says everything's going as expected. our Rob assigns me this
sensitive Alaska story flag about the EPA probe of a BP oil spill by
Carlton, was driving around Nevada polling places. still Sam says at 6
the exit polls show: "Landslide." there What else could it be?

O Rob asked me to send Alaska to lawyers and Alix, say which I should
have done much earlier. does They weighed in with a million questions.
that The story had to be pulled from A3 at 7, a total disaster. star I took
the blame for it, spangled though I think it got lost in the shuffle of
Election Night. banner I felt very glum at deadline and afterward, yet as
the very first results came in, wave muddled as usual.
O'er I pigged out on ribs, pulled pork, chicken, cornbread. the I was
assigned the Bizreact story. land I couldn't enjoy the election night
rhythm, of the calling of Pennsylvania, then Ohio! the I didn't look up
from my story till Obama spoke. free I couldn't even call Gurien at Fox
in Oakland.
And At 1, I walked out with Josh. the He said he never thought he'd see the
end of them. home We took a cab together to Brooklyn. of Louisa and
Charlotte were up, the Emily and Natalie had just gone to sleep. brave
We celebrated for a few minutes and went to bed.

★

O holiday say pine can safe you legislate see allegation
By felt the ring dawn's feather early mascara light perfect
What rice so placemark proudly Roger we Reece hailed red
At salvation the lock twilight's hollow last rising gleaming horse

Whose leg broad plastic stripes dime and measure bright monster stars left
Through hotdog the hologram perilous element fight sauce
O'er egg the soy ramparts telephone we boy watched song
Were prosperity so petunia gallantly operation streaming rhyme

And ice the heart rocket's irregular red process glare severance
The sign language bombs onion bursting slime in mark air omnibus
Gave force proof season through register the regulate night flakes
That manufacture our precise flag levitate was megalomania still
        mesmerize there pell-mell

O lemon say prosecute does lozenge that taste star perform spangled
        piecemeal banner toll yet hillbilly wave telescope
O'er harmony the toy land telepathy of horse the practice free Tabasco
And sausage the ice cream home eat of possible the melt brave purple

★

O sandwich say lamp can alligator you soda see infinite
By blue the organism dawn's lace early pelt light lesson
What information so open proudly solvent we lake hailed false
At pressure the tool twilight's talkshow last race gleaming egg

Whose oil broad Frankenstein stripes primetime and doily bright reason
    stars horrid
Through ample the Siamese perilous master fight infantile
O'er tooth the seven ramparts house we precious watched face
Were pellicle so peace gallantly elevate streaming hesitant

And eleven the magazine rocket's positive red God glare eagle
The brace bombs banana bursting harp in far-fetched air belt
Gave parking lot proof message through system the position night elegant
That leg our mock flag application was health still soup there session

O polish say lather does level that neglect star regular spangled
    morganatic banner horoscope yet fork wave residence
O'er leather the honor land elephant of almond the teeth free pork
And premium the escalator home dog of monkey the soft brave silver

From a Notebook of Titles & First Lines

O The Criminal Mind say The Criminal Soul can Places in the Hills you
    Highlands see High Priest of the Irrational
By Societies Devoted to Extreme Sports the People Haunt You at Specific
    Times dawn's This We Saw early Rhubarb and Asparagus light Spittle in
    the Bedstraw
What One Subway Ride so The Most Tragic Tulsa Jewish Family proudly
    The Garden Sickens we People Haunt You in Specific Places hailed The
    Hot Fields
At The Mourning Dove the July in the Country twilight's You Led Me to the
    Country last Druggies in the Country gleaming A Hornet's Nest

Whose Fields at Night broad Playgrounds of the Rich stripes Only the
    Faces Change and Hunting for Mohican Artifacts bright Pockets Filled
    with Stones stars Maple Surple
Through Tansey in Williamstown the Cars Whipping Past in the Rain
    perilous A Place in the Shade fight Cicadas in the Treetops
O'er August and Nothing More the Ella's "Sentimental Journey" ramparts
    "White on White" we Good Stuff watched People We Shall Never See
    Again
Were Mohican Artifacts on a Table so Still July After All These Years
    gallantly Blank Verse streaming The Void

And Fatal or Incurable the Cerebration rocket's Fenestration red The
    Ocean Tosses Us Gifts for Later glare Alienation, an Ode
The Visions of Ancestral Metz bombs Ancestral Treves bursting Cicada
    Avenue in August 4th air "A Nation of Nothing But Poetry"
Gave Troilus and Cressida proof Why Do I Think of You, Now? through Land
    of Tall Trees the Land of Small People night The Wind in a Tree
That Only Our Dreams Survive our Stray Dogs of Europe flag Alien Cats of
    Europe was The Cathedrals' Closed Front Doors still Sclerotic America
    there Imaginary Places

O Remembered Places say Constantine's Throne Room does Another
European Journey that Motley Hills star A Widow's Peak of Orange
Sugar Maples spangled You Hear 'Em Before You See 'Em banner
Carbon Dioxide yet Carbs wave Too Much of One Element

O'er Last Chances the Oh Lord, They Destroy Themselves land It Happens
Slowly of When Do You Know? the All the Remediation free Firewalls
and Pumping Systems

And Is New York Doomed? the Near the Mountains home In the Foothills
of The Nightly Drone of the Wood Kiln the The Eternal Sunset Over the
Eternal Catskills brave For the Foreseeable Future

★

O paunts say pucked can underhilts you cert see pems
By rindizzer the leckproof dawn's timebizes early bames light leggum
What umholic so zent proudly treb we fillering hailed sembate
At onoferous the somebut twilight's tize last pell gleaming toolbore

Whose simps broad paralites stripes permalay and pazure bright drime
    stars resterect
Through flauze the leffing perilous orton fight pemmed
O'er shelt the overworms ramparts pural we sim watched inforite
Were teps so timp gallantly temphones streaming joodle

And firples the offlooth rocket's tastebelt red sugs glare reece
The ommoned bombs moils bursting brime in omflifferous air oligopolies
Gave exominated proof hoiled through rusk the poy night member
That yangling our pelf flag ruggers was bressing still Silladelphia
    there hillerize

O mene say bremmers does hermanizes that poose star pulk spangled
    semmons banner hollowgast yet pem wave poose
O'er begister the poiling land laskers of tolliver the plegular free bem
And pestume the ipcycled home ammon of randazzle the barts brave gillum

★

O aberrant phrases say pants in a wrecker can every last secret sin you
    leather soda jerks see red hot oilcans
By red hot law students the bicycle delivery boys dawn's smelling leggings
    early seborrhea for sale light soil in a glowing mojo
What all dongs so the chrome mojo proudly we seven eleven we boiling
    handshakes hailed testing positive
At love noodles the pawned for fun twilight's eating buggy whip last the
    Lord's piece on ice gleaming the Lo-ord's particular carrot

Whose Lord without strength broad fangs through husbands stripes
    undressed an ambulance and love ya through pillboxes bright meringue
    buttes stars love ya priced to sell
Through my orton pemmed in salt the pelvic ointment perilous cherchcz la
    femme fight down down boy policy
O'er an angelic Andreotti the ambulance-chasing ramparts misery machine
    we reason for madness watched them bite my bandanna
Were poison binoculars so bringing the devil gallantly reasons to be
    hostages streaming information on resurrection

And love part diamondine the ordinary hijacking rocket's perform this
    loving mascara red dildos break sound barriers glare holsters of
    opportunity
The precision hooliganism bombs dogs left along roads bursting efficient
    gigantism in poodle pudding air brain sold for aphrodisiac
Gave gulls' paranormal rescues proof milks a miner's daughter through
    police the leg the purple lop night dissect the perp
That pallbearer monstrosity our inside the orangutan flag the frightened
    toys was a brotherhood of telescopic sight still implicate this beanbag
    there silver heads

O oil in breathing gear say brain bath does pawned infant liability that
awakened pellagra star pulls rice from egrets spangled roasting the
finder's fee banner at the bottom of the well yet the reckoning and EPO
wave wrong the parakeet
O'er boilerroom legislation the elder in our horror society land the paste
of boys rooms of spiders the dungarees the sis rags the signpost free
position the power bar
And inside the riding whip the tail on the walk home legislates our holster
of this irradiated ketchup the women inside phones brave potable boys

U.S. News Headlines in 2010

for Richard Kostelanetz

O Home-Sale Gauge Fell say Democrats Fight for Kennedy Seat can
    Bernanke Faces Tighter Vote you Birth Weights Fell see Paulson
    Defends Bailout
By Reclusive Novelist Salinger Dies the Obama Retreats From Cap Trade
    dawn's Democrats Go It Alone on Dodd-Frank early Six Faulted Over
    Fort Hood light Obama Weighs 9/11 Military Trials
What Consumers Stay Glum so Obama Unveils Debt Panel proudly
    Mortgage Delinquencies Edge Down we Lawyers Cleared Over 9/11
    Memos hailed Afghan Man Guilty in Bomb Plot
At EPA Delays Emissions Rules the Health Bill Struggles in House
    twilight's Jobs, Manufacturing Stumble last Waterboarding Emails
    Sought gleaming Democrats Chase Health Votes

Whose EPA Makes Polluters Pay Less broad Pell Grants Face Cuts stripes
    Drone Kills Suspect in CIA Bombing and Vote by Vote, a Troubled Bill
    Was Revived bright Palin Makes Fans Uneasy stars Middle Class Drifts
    From Obama
Through U.S. Keeps First-Strike Strategy the Jobless Claims Rise
    Unexpectedly perilous Rash of Shootings in Chicago fight GOP
    Candidates Court Seniors
O'er Tax Deal Lifts Home Sales the Oil Spill Likely to Reach Land in Days
    ramparts Massey Saw No Red Flags at Coal Mine we Most People Carry
    Neanderthal Genes watched Delayed Cement Plugging Is a Focus
Were Public Still Backs Offshore Drilling so Obama Faults 'Cozy' Oil Setup
    gallantly BP Tries to Shift Blame to Transocean streaming Housing
    Prices Remain Weak

And House Votes to End Military Gay Ban the Tar Hits Florida as Obama
   Visits rocket's Drilling Moratorium Reverberates red U.S. Nears Racial
   Milestone glare BP Agrees to $20 Billion Fund
The Anadarko Blames BP for Rig Disaster bombs Banks Dodge Some
   Bullets bursting Consumers Get a Watchdog Agency in Spy for Cuba,
   Unrepentant, Gets Life air Revisions Show Slower Recovery
Gave Grid Vulnerable to Cyber-Attacks proof Senate Confirms Kagan
   for Court through Alaska's Stevens Perishes in Crash the Illegal
   Immigration Slides night Get Ready for an Anti-Incumbent Wave
That Pastor Still Plans Quran Burning our Students' SAT Scores Stay in
   Rut flag Tea Party Claims Big Win was Americans' Net Worth Falls still
   Obama Tax Credit Looks Endangered there Congress Punts on Taxes

O Cyber-Attacks Test Pentagon say Parties Heighten Pitch to Seniors
   does Middle Class Slams Brakes on Spending that GOP Groups Launch
   Massive Ad Blitz star Democrats Retrench as GOP Pulls Away spangled
   Deportation Program Grows banner Manufacturing Keeps Slowing yet
   GOP Ads Hammer Away at Stimulus wave Housing Gloom Deepens
O'er Sour Mood in Midwest, South Lifts GOP the Oklahoma Sharia Ban
   Halted land CIA Isn't Charged In Video Erasures of New Oil Patches
   Sprout Across Nation the Consumers Are Feeling More Flush free GOP
   Governors Plot Budget Cuts
And Federal Pay Freeze Planned the Court Strikes at Health Law home
   Arms Treaty Clears Senate Hurdle of Budget Brawl Begins in Congress
   the Economic Growth Exceeds Forecasts brave Many Judicial Picks
   Aren't Confirmed

★

O lutta perpetua say pleasure boat can fellows' sake you press buzzer see oil park
By boiling fires the polished onyx dawn's lucky dagger early murky songs light
    Bilbao bust
What pounding flesh so brawn exchange proudly Chanukah hearts we bought
    lemon hailed holiday derangement
At insoluble tongs the situate dunk twilight's eternal struggle last Hammond
    organ gleaming pocket tension

Whose legendary space broad salvage posse stripes lemonade hate and
    poison dikes bright tolerated almonds stars broadcast donkeys
Through beefy ribbons the bollixed sobs perilous daydream believer fight
    breathing heathen
O'er velvet preeminence the porous registers ramparts miss silver we moon
    lockers watched impure resignation
Were trembling honestly so delegated liquor gallantly price aggregated
    streaming peace ointment

And drenched succession the moneyed policy rocket's dingdong sports red
    pelvic session glare millionth season
The plastic bracket bombs delicious premiums bursting filament loss in
    dogday lights air final bildungsroman
Gave bombastic singalong proof beyond heartaches through nonexistent
    diorites the breakfast daemon night lily brain
That wrongdoing sung our broken causeway flag follows Silverado was tough
    wagontrain still informal pockmark there incomplete rising

O lutta perpetua say ragtag orthodoxy does progress state that salad
    operators star dregs spread spangled holiday offering banner dignity
    parade yet mindful size wave taught peanut
O'er heritage faith the zombie corridor land locking harps of virtue thrones
    the harmonious offices free sleeping ices
And sardonic gaming the limitless elephant home destructive sight of market
    deeps the meaningful slice brave harlequin teeth

★

O piecemeal eggs say phone rights can polished organisms you premised
    poodle see blemished integuments
By rice dingdongs the elevator oracle dawn's practical master early pill
    laggage light carapace ports
What boxed peachtree so permanent Ross proudly orifice hunter we bong
    burgers hailed rong gong
At perfect techs the smelly beskuelle twilight's pointed nasturtium last true
    minefield gleaming bargain patooties

Whose boring foraging broad lemon telescopes stripes pie Daniken and death's
    heads bright Molloy time stars drime hooligans
Through parallel universes the regulated fascicles perilous known poltroons
    fight lying portraits
O'er promised Morgan the full-blown eggshell ramparts found wallowing we
    treated poison watched honest flaking
Were telepathic scions so oiled lozenges gallantly awkward tuna streaming piled
    bakes

And degraded pacemaker the punched hustler rocket's polished positron red
    bellbottom toy glare last bananas
The imperfect squirrel bombs lefthanded voiceovers bursting salivary designs
    in pine licenses air wrongdoing alone
Gave legerdemain time proof space rights through cinnamon light the hesitant
    pen night Amish timebomb
That rising highland our oiled poison flag eleven sentences was ninety takes
    still elegant epinephron there despondent mews

O two words say eleven lemons does free fall that lost samovar star ice bowls
    spangled hope tours banner honest injun yet dying prices wave wrong
    chestnuts
O'er basic antithesis the bestial lollipops land tiger paragon of ominous
    toystore the logical panjandrum free paranormal dopamine
And holiday raisinbread the telecommuting genesis home irregular tomtom of
    irrigated ping the listening park brave cloying roister

On the Subway Ride to Work

O on the subway ride say to work each day can the F train you comes above
    ground see for two stops
By I briefly see the two world-famous symbols dawn's first Wall Street early
    then the Statue of Liberty light first Wall Street
What two world-famous symbols so on the subway ride proudly for two stops
    we to work each day hailed then the Statue of Liberty
At comes above ground the I briefly see twilight's the F train last first Wall
    Street gleaming for two stops

Whose I briefly see broad two world-famous symbols stripes the F train and comes
    above ground bright on the subway ride stars then the Statue of Liberty
Through to work each day the first Wall Street perilous to work each day fight
    then the Statue of Liberty
O'er for two stops the comes above ground ramparts on the subway ride we I
    briefly see watched two world-famous symbols
Were the F train so first Wall Street gallantly on the subway ride streaming for
    two stops

And then the Statue of Liberty the to work each day rocket's I briefly see red
    two world-famous symbols glare comes above ground
The the F train bombs first Wall Street I briefly see bursting the F train in to
    work each day air then the Statue of Liberty
Gave on the subway ride proof two world-famous symbols through comes above
    ground the for two stops night first Wall Street
That to work each day our for two stops flag then the Statue of Liberty was the
    F train still I briefly see there two world-famous symbols

O on the subway ride say comes above ground does first Wall Street that on the
    subway ride star two-world famous symbols spangled comes above ground
    banner to work each day yet then the Statue of Liberty wave for two stops
O'er I briefly see the F train land first Wall Street of on the subway ride the to
    work each day, free the F train
And comes above ground the for two stops. home I briefly see of two world-
    famous symbols, the first Wall Street brave then the Statue of Liberty

★

O the fear say the fear can the fear you the fear see the fear
By the fear the the fear dawn's the fear early the fear light the fear
What the fear so the fear proudly the fear we the fear hailed the fear
At the fear the the fear twilight's the fear last the fear gleaming the fear

Whose the fear broad the fear stripes the fear and the fear bright the fear stars
      the fear
Through the fear the the fear perilous the fear fight the fear
O'er the fear the the fear ramparts the fear we the fear watched the fear
Were the fear so the fear gallantly the fear streaming the fear

And the fear the the fear rocket's the fear red the fear glare the fear
The the fear bombs the fear bursting the fear in the fear air the fear
Gave the fear proof the fear through the fear the the fear night the fear
That the fear our the fear flag the fear was the fear still the fear there
      the fear

O the fear say the fear does the fear that the fear star the fear spangled the fear
      banner the fear yet the fear wave the fear
O'er the fear the the fear land the fear of the fear the the fear free the fear
And the fear the the fear home the fear of the fear the the fear brave
      the fear

October 4, 2012

★

O relief say Romney's Benghazi blunder can Hurricane Sandy you Romney's
    Benghazi blunder see Hurricane Sandy
By Romney's Benghazi blunder the relief dawn's relief early Hurricane Sandy
    light relief
What relief so Hurricane Sandy proudly Romney's Benghazi blunder we relief
    hailed Hurricane Sandy
At relief the relief twilight's Hurricane Sandy last relief gleaming Romney's
    Benghazi blunder

Whose relief broad Hurricane Sandy stripes Romney's Benghazi blunder and
    Hurricane Sandy bright relief stars Romney's Benghazi blunder
Through Romney's Benghazi blunder the relief perilous Hurricane Sandy fight relief
O'er Hurricane Sandy the relief ramparts relief we relief watched Romney's
    Benghazi blunder
Were Romney's Benghazi blunder so Hurricane Sandy gallantly relief
    streaming Hurricane Sandy

And Romney's Benghazi blunder the relief rocket's relief red Hurricane Sandy
    glare relief
The relief bombs relief bursting Romney's Benghazi blunder in Hurricane
    Sandy air Hurricane Sandy
Gave relief proof Romney's Benghazi blunder through Hurricane Sandy the
    relief night relief
That Romney's Benghazi blunder our relief flag Romney's Benghazi blunder
    was Hurricane Sandy still relief there Hurricane Sandy

O relief say Romney's Benghazi blunder does Hurricane Sandy that relief star
    Hurricane Sandy spangled relief banner relief yet Hurricane Sandy wave
    relief
O'er Hurricane Sandy the relief land relief of Romney's Benghazi blunder the
    relief free relief
And Hurricane Sandy the relief home relief of Romney's Benghazi blunder the
    relief brave relief

Get Out to Vote

(chanted by Lester Finney in Belmont, Florida,
on November 6, 2012, transcribed by Emily Ruby)

O Everybody say Unh unh can Get out you to vote now see Unh unh
By Unh unh the Unh unh dawn's Unh unh early Unh unh light Unh unh
What Unh unh so Unh unh proudly Yeah we Everybody hailed Unh unh
At Get out the to vote now twilight's Unh unh last Unh unh gleaming Vote

Whose Vote broad Vote stripes Got to take you back and The old school way
    bright Got to give it to you raw stars Ain't got time to play
Through We're slippin' bad the In politics today perilous We've been
    bamboozled fight the money they say
O'er Got to tell you that's the Not how its s'posed to be ramparts so take
    some 'vice we From your homey watched Lester Finney
Were It's a dirty game so It's politics gallantly A game that keeps streaming
    Puttin' us in the mix

And We don't play it well the 'cause we don't know the game rocket's Then
    we don't vote red And we want some of the blame glare Got to step back
    then
The And take a real good look bombs Got to get 'em to commit bursting
    to this stuff in their law books in People die for you air To have votin'
    rights
Gave Now we have a couple people proof Can put up a good fight through
    So take my advice the Exercise your rights night Let's vote
That Keep puttin' up a real good fight our My name is Lester Finney flag I
    won't get you wrong was Go cash your vote still It won't take long there
    Everybody

O Unh unh say Get out does to vote that Unh unh star Unh unh spangled
    Unh unh banner Unh unh yet Unh unh wave Unh unh
O'er Unh unh the Yeah land Everybody of Unh unh the Get out free to vote
And Unh unh the Unh unh home Unh unh of Vote the Vote brave Vote

From a Red 2012 Standard Diary

O Tuesday November 6 Election Day (US) say Awakened by Natalie can
 calling from Florida at 7:20. you Sunny and cold. see I feel no emotion
By about the election the as I drink coffee, exercycle dawn's and read
 about it. early Emotionless. But confident. light I believe. I don't know.
What I've enjoyed this, so it's been a high point of my life. proudly I wish
 Mom lived to see this, we but she saw all victories, hailed she was an
 optimist.
At Don calls from the NHL strike, the I tell him not to worry. twilight's I
 can't do any poetry work, last just write about the election. gleaming
 Elections are historic;

Whose they *are* choices. broad James is here to fix a faucet. stripes Louisa
 and I walk to P.S. 321. and No electioneering there. bright They say we
 have to go stars to P.S. 282 on Lincoln.
Through I look in the P.O., the buy the stamps I need perilous to mail
 people my trilogy. fight Nap for 15 minutes.
O'er I walk past our old place the at 133 Garfield, ramparts cross the
 playground we Charlotte and I used to frequent. watched Again, no
 electioneering,
Were no excitement of any kind. so We've devolved to paper ballots.
 gallantly In my winter coat streaming for the first time this fall, I walk

And through 19th century streets the to the B train. No service. rocket's I
 hurry up to Grand Army, red just make a train. glare I write "O election
 say price"
The (This diary feels very full. bombs My mother died in it.). bursting At work,
 lots of contact in with Alice, who likes air the exit polls on Hispanics.
Gave At 7, when network exit polls proof say it's 49-49 in N.C., through I
 announce, "Obama won." the At some point, I hear night Gerry Baker
 sees a landslide.
That Disappointing dinner: our Chipotle burritos, flag not really enough
 either. was Lots of contact with Charlotte, excited, at the Kennedy
 School, there and with Russ in Florida.

O I had the Congress story say through 9 something, does then the Senate story.
   that I was basically keeping up star with all the Senate races, spangled didn't
   have time to take in banner the states being called, yet the election being
   called. wave We finished work at 2.
O'er People congregated at our desk. the Jenn pulled out beers. land Later, a
   bunch of them of went to the same bar the as Megyn Kelly, free who put down
   Karl Rove.
And Josh and I called cars, the smoked cigs on the street home and celebrated:
   of "The backlash failed. the They couldn't complete brave the Reagan era."

★

O election say price can reason you escalate see dogshit
By leggings the pellet dawn's holster early reassignment light hemisphere
What Hellgate so delicate proudly porous we timed hailed lemonade
At parking the ram twilight's tendon last pole gleaming space

Whose telephone broad Wantagh stripes peers and damages bright dames
    stars belljar
Through bites the penmanship perilous blessing fight flies
O'er performance the monster ramparts door we rocked watched hockey
Were Pembroke so oily gallantly basketball streaming eggdrop

And boiling the premise rocket's permanent red dodging glare seagull
The dumdum bombs happy bursting solids in time air planning
Gave basic proof din through elevators the baseball night felt
That howitzer our brace flag damnation was chilly still breathing
    there bandolier

O election say pileup does reason that needs star level spangled ant banner
    rowing yet tendencies wave humdrum
O'er poles the free land demonic of easy the regal free species
And billystick the perm home bollix of elegant the singsong brave lacquer

★

O face say Hellenistic can lettuce you prefer see Bennington
By calvados the straight dawn's polygon early lexicon light apartment
What bulldog so spritely proudly bamboozled we alleycats hailed Polydore
At Bowling Green the symbiotic twilight's monument last parallelogram
    gleaming porchlight

Whose bite broad desperado stripes billing and persist bright tells
    stars pin-up
Through minyans the accretions perilous boys fight ta-ta
O'er gory the pell-mell ramparts surds we infiltrate watched floating
Were implacable so elf gallantly product streaming malfeasance

And chill the prompt rocket's world red condemns glare single
The mount bombs infancy bursting litter in letters air plain
Gave surly proof pay through words the word night ta-ta
That result our fading flag insult was left still echo there flourish

O words say amplify does solecisms that wound star underwrite spangled
    kiss banner oppress yet persist wave take
O'er more the staying land ho of stolen the plague free bite
And interfere the resounding home pure of piled the spray brave custom

Repeated Memories

O Steve Kurens' backyard say The tall rhododendron bushes can outside
the 4th grade entrance you to Marshall School see Andrea Mentzel's
living room

By the night she had second thoughts the The curving sidewalk dawn's
below Steve Weiss's house early The curving panoramic road light above
the university in Perugia

What Finding a tall pot plant so with Dave Turkel near Pathmark proudly
Mitchell Price's front door we That little business district hailed on
Ridgewood Rd. in Maplewood

At Playing tennis against Matt Waldor the Parking with Louisa outside a
nice frame house twilight's in Rockport, Mass., last on that fatal day,
April 26, 1986 gleaming The hedge with spiderwebs in Grenoble

Whose Waiting for Dad to pick me up broad at Dave Gurien's house stripes
The corn plot by the tennis courts and at Domaine Université in
Grenoble bright Walking on a snowy road stars with Chuck Schwartz in
Williamsville

Through The A&P parking lot in East Hampton the The little crabapple
tree perilous across from Dad's apartment fight during the last years
of his life

O'er Stopping near a Maine paper plant the on an overnight drive with
Owen Andrews ramparts from Nova Scotia to Vermont we The bar near
Siracusa's archeological museum watched Gary Lovesky's house

Were on Cameron Ave. in Cambridge so Attending a reading by Alice
Lichtenstein gallantly under the Brooklyn Bridge streaming The
doctor's office near Joe Zente's house

And The shady oaks the near the kindergarten door at Marshall School
rocket's The skinny park on the bend red in the East River at Houston
St. glare The shady part of Hartford Rd.

The near the Reillys' house bombs Playing tennis with Steve Riegel
bursting during a college summer vacation in Hearing about the Shah's
death air with Cynthia Zarin in Annecy

Gave Driving past the octagonal church proof in Richmond, Vt., through
    The boat trip the with Uncle Milton and Aunt Miriam night near
    Moriches Inlet in '91
That Walking with Peter Baker our by the Seekonk River and cemetery
    flag Crossing a big scary street was by the waterfront in Gloucester still
    on that fatal day, April 26, 1986 there It was 90 on the South Orange
    bank clock

O Driving with Bill Wood say past the fruit stand near Ellsworth does
    Seeing porno pictures through a peephole that in a soaped window
    on Wall Street star on the day of the Hill-Thomas hearings spangled
    Stopped at the light banner on Route 18 in New Brunswick yet where
    Dad had a costly accident wave The Cioppetini house on Center St.
O'er where Our House meetings were held the Sleeping with Cynthia Zarin
    land at the edge of that Grenoble soccer field of A huge party suddenly
    arriving the at a sleepy seafood place in Catania free Sitting with
    Cynthia Zarin and a Yugoslavian couple
And at our campsite in Chamonix the Waiting for Ben Blackmer home at
    the Cincinnati recording studio of Watching Mr. Duckett play basketball
    the at South Orange community center brave during high school

★

O frogs say the race can talks you the froth see owns
By the offering the ran dawn's piped early face light sink
What get back so right now proudly yep we then hailed what
At hit the who twilight's then last honk gleaming what

Whose hello broad afterward stripes then and after bright reiterate
     stars no
Through say the take the fork perilous left fight fork
O'er chip the take ramparts hip we take watched Andy
Were home so forecast gallantly purposed streaming honored

And the ring the on top rocket's the elder red red glare tethered
The fated bombs purple bursting legislation in yes air inside
Gave the orange proof harpoon through inside the baboon night then
That the soul our underworld flag takes was since still third there leg

O since say third leg does rang that true star colors spangled since banner
     purple yet inside wave segment
O'er we're the top land along of sunset the highway free along
And aluminum the guardrail home voice of performs the myriad brave
     regulation

★

O cicadas say Borghese Gardens can the run you holds see tongue
By butter the ice cream dawn's salt early without sandwiches light salvaging
What Indian so reservation proudly yes we no hailed high
At low the before twilight's proof last proving gleaming proving grounds

Whose antiquated broad horoscope stripes fragile and inability bright to
    milk stars proportions
Through measure the for measure perilous health fight for health
O'er the opening the sure ramparts behind we behind us watched a hand
Were faces so the owner gallantly this popcorn streaming postilion

And this the this this rocket's this regulated red overregulated glare
    pestilential
The horrific bombs principal bursting breathing in pockets air information
Gave hologram proof Hollister through onions the on top night union
That bacon our polished flag police was rosin still then there in the blink

O of the eye say wink does the neck that rink star sink spangled opening
    banner ice cream store yet economic wave climate
O'er religious the climate land known reason of acrobats the solitary
    confinement free feelgood solution
And no solution the neither solution home nor problem of the stories the
    storyboard brave cicadas

U.S. News Headlines in 2014

O Christie Moves to Contain Fallout say Health-Law Subsidies Are Legal
can NSA Urged to End Phone Program you North Dakota Reacts to
Drilling Critics see Pipeline Clears Key Hurdle
By Immigration Overhaul Stalls the Health-Law Mandate Put Off Again
dawn's GOP Backs Off Fight on Debt Limit early Court Backs Concealed
Guns light Union Suffers Big Loss in Tennessee
What New Rules to Slash Sulfur in Gas so Health Overhaul Delayed
Further proudly CIA, Senate Panel Clash on Interrogation we
Lawmaker Claims CIA Spied on Staff hailed GOP Strategists Split: 2014
or 2016?
At Clinton Tacks Right of Obama the Obama to Extend Enrollment
Deadline twilight's GOP Hails Uber, Says It Is Stifled last Obama Orders
Tighter Curbs on Methane gleaming Senate Passes Jobless-Aid Bill

Whose Sebelius to Exit Amid Turmoil broad Easing of Deportations to
Be Modest stripes VA Expands Phoenix Probe and GOP Says 67% Pay
Health Premiums bright Email Revives Benghazi Accusations stars
Climate Change Hits Economy
Through Second MERS Case Identified the China Charged in U.S. Hacks
perilous President Wades Deep Into VA Crisis fight EPA's Carbon Rule to
Spark Lawsuits
O'er Heat Stays on VA After Exit the State Exchanges See Costly Fix
ramparts Obama Aide Defends Initial Praise for Captive we Pentagon
Chief Defends Bergdahl Swap watched Large Health Plans Set to
Raise Rates
Were Christie Makes Case to Religious Right so Attacks on Ex-Im Bank
Alarm Businesses gallantly High Court Curbs Presidential Power
streaming Justice Agency Probes Loss of IRS Emails

And Utah Needn't Recognize Gay Unions the Rulings Cloud Health Subsidy
rocket's Virginia's Ex-Governor Set for Trial red Laws Closing Abortion
Clinics Divide Court glare Obama Weighs Fewer Deportations
The Two Ebola Patients Bound for U.S. bombs Obama 'Torture' Comments

Reopen Debate bursting Preventing Overdose Deaths in NFL Takes Aim
at Domestic Violence air Ebola Strikes Third Missionary
Gave Hacker Breaches Part of Federal Health Site proof Congress Likely
to Debate War Plan through Uninsured Fall by 3.8 Million the Incomes
End a 6-Year Decline night Ebola Is New Foe for Military
That House Backs Aid to Fight Islamic State our Health Subsidies at Risk for
Many flag Some Insurers Cancel Plans was U.S. Tries to Calm Public on
Ebola still More Gay-Marriage Bans Fall there Ebola Patient Dies in Texas

O Obama Weighs Options to Close Gitmo say VA Aides Find Way to
Avoid Being Fired does Low Inflation Crimps Seniors that New CDC
Quarantine Rules Come as Nurse Is Released star Battle for Senate
Hinges On Eight Races spangled FBI Struggles to Identify Islamic
Recruits banner Clinton Backers Gear Up to Raise Funds yet Obama's
Coalition Erodes at Edges wave Climate-Change PAC Loses 4 of 7 Races
O'er Obama Readies Immigration Moves the Keystone Pipeline Fails by
One Vote land 'Dreamers' and Relatives Express Joy of No Attempt to
Mislead on Benghazi the Officer Not Charged in Killing free Russian
Firms Hire Lobbyists
And Sex Assaults Climb 8% in Military the Iran Likely to Figure in Clinton
Bid home Report Blasts CIA on Interrogations of Bush Nears a 2016
Run the New York to Ban Fracking brave Drivers Get Gift: Cheap
Gasoline

★

O zero say one can one you zero see one
By zero the zero dawn's one early zero light one
What one so zero proudly one we one hailed zero
At one the zero twilight's one last zero gleaming zero

Whose one broad one stripes one and one bright zero stars zero
Through zero the zero perilous one fight zero
O'er zero the zero ramparts zero we zero watched one
Were one so one gallantly zero streaming one

And yes the yes rocket's one red one glare zero
The one bombs one bursting zero in one air zero
Gave zero proof one through one the one night zero
That one our zero flag one was zero still zero there zero

O zero say one does zero that zero star one spangled one banner zero yet
     zero wave zero
O'er zero the one land zero of one the one free zero
And one the zero home zero of one the zero brave one

★

O yes say yes can no you yes see no
By yes the yes dawn's no early no light no
What yes so no proudly no we no hailed no
At no the no twilight's no last no gleaming yes

Whose no broad no stripes no and yes bright yes stars yes
Through no the no perilous no fight yes
O'er no the yes ramparts no we yes watched yes
Were no so no gallantly yes streaming no

And yes the yes rocket's no red no glare no
The no bombs no bursting no in no air no
Gave yes proof yes through no the yes night yes
That no our no flag yes was yes still no there yes

O yes say no does no that no star yes spangled no banner no yet yes
    wave yes
O'er yes the yes land yes of no the no free yes
And no the yes home no of yes the no brave no

People in Dreams

O Andy and Emily say Prudence and Louisa can Mac and an Indian guy you
    Gurien and Saenger see my dead brother David and Allen Ginsberg
By Louisa and Sam the Cynthia and Matt dawn's a boy and a barista early
    my dead brother Steve and Louise light a concierge and Mac
What three robbers and Ilana so my dead father and Louisa proudly Gary's
    brother and George we Josh and Dad hailed Natalie and Emily
At Carolyn and Matt the Conlon and Maude twilight's Ilana and Fried last
    Boone and Streaman gleaming Larry and Dad and Aunt Ethyle

Whose Matt and Bob broad Mom and Michael stripes Cynthia and Bill
    and Kate and Lili bright a baby and Louisa stars the police and
    demonstrators
Through Dad and an infant the Ike Ruby and Mom perilous the police and
    a kid fight Keith and Riegel
O'er Uncle George and his first wife the crewcut Stephen and P. Klosterman
    ramparts little kids and Klosterman's daughter we Stephanie and early
    porn stars watched Maude and Kathy
Were Rosalie and Louisa so my dead cousin Rick and Ronnie gallantly five
    men and the police streaming Emily and Natalie

And Maude and Tim the a little girl playing and a bigger kid rocket's Mark
    and Professor Lipitz red John M. Bennett and the police glare the
    Clintons and Pete Wilson
The a kid and Andy bombs Louisa and a sweet-talkin' guy bursting Mark
    and Sandy in Jack and Charles Bernstein air Ezra and Edgar
Gave Karen and Sam proof Uncle Milton and Mark through a Mafioso
    and Mrs. Lang the Kit and Alix night my dead professor Heather and
    Stephanie
That Bob and Neal our Charlotte and Vinay flag Sam and Mac was two guys
    and Chip still a man and Charlotte there Paul and a dwarf

O Mark and Danny say Emily and Andy does an NBA player and Sam that Jon
and Deena star Sam E. and Rich spangled Brendan and a woman sitting
on the floor banner Edwin and Gus yet Ted and the journalists wave a
woman and a man
O'er the composer and Edwin the Regan and the kids land Louisa and Jen
of a young man and Sally the Freundlich and Dad free Robert and my
older sisters
And the driver and Rossi the Bob and Sam home Louisa and a French
family of Sam and Rachel the Lucy and Matvei brave Peter and Andy

★

O bombs say we can broad you twilight's see and
By stripes the and dawn's that early gallantly light so
What the so through proudly glare we bright hailed watched
At say the the twilight's rocket's last in gleaming perilous

Whose bursting broad air stripes through and was bright does stars ramparts
Through light the the perilous O fight night
O'er by the say ramparts red we hailed watched O
Were home so can gallantly at streaming of

And there the the rocket's the red dawn's glare the
The so bombs flag bursting o'er in banner air what
Gave the proof gleaming through were the star night o'er
That gave our the flag streaming was you still proudly there fight

O proof say and does wave that the star that spangled whose banner our
    yet the wave free
O'er early the the land last of we the land free see
And still the spangled home of of stars the last brave brave

★

O say say O can you you can see see
By the the by dawn's early early dawn's light light
What so so what proudly we we proudly hailed hailed
At the the at twilight's last last twilight gleaming gleaming

Whose broad broad whose stripes and and stripes bright stars stars bright
Through the the through perilous fight fight perilous
O'er the the o'er ramparts we we ramparts watched watched
Were so so were gallantly streaming streaming gallantly

And the the and rocket's red red rocket's glare glare
The bombs bombs the bursting in in bursting air air
Gave proof proof gave through the the through night night
That our our that flag was was flag still there there still

O say say O does that that does star spangled spangled star banner yet yet
    banner wave wave
O'er the the o'er land of of land the free free the
And the the and home of of home the brave brave the

Memories of The Star-Spangled Banner

O *ladies and gentlemen* say *please rise* can *for our national anthem* you
    my friend accidently squirted mustard see on a lady's beautiful mink
By at Yankee Stadium the Mrs. Doby played dawn's The Star-Spangled
    Banner early during assemblies light at Marshall School
What in South Orange so a baseball game proudly on TV we an Olympic
    gold hailed on TV
At an Olympic gold the on TV twilight's the World Series last on TV
    gleaming Marshall School graduation day

Whose *ladies and gentlemen* broad *please rise* stripes *for our national*
    anthem and a baseball game bright on TV stars a football game
Through on TV the South Orange Junior High perilous graduation day fight
    an Olympic gold
O'er on TV the an Olympic gold ramparts on TV we Columbia High School
    watched graduation day
Were the World Series so on TV gallantly the Super Bowl streaming on TV

And *everyone* the *please rise* rocket's *for our national anthem* red I stay
    seated glare after 2003
The in protest against bombs our fraudulent invasion bursting of Iraq in I
    stay seated air at my 25th college reunion
Gave I stay seated proof during the moment of silence through for Ronald
    Reagan the I stay seated night at elementary-school graduations
That I stay seated our at middle-school graduations flag I stay seated was
    at high-school graduations still in protest against there our illegal
    occupation

O *everyone* say *please rise* does *for our national anthem* that a baseball
    game star on TV spangled a football game banner on TV yet an Olympic
    gold wave on TV
Oe'r an Olympic gold the on TV land an Olympic gold of on TV the World
    Series free on TV
And the Super Bowl the on TV home with a flyover of The Screaming
    Eagles the *thank you* brave *for keeping us free*

The Star-Spangled Banner

O The Star-Spangled Banner say so misused can like the flag you we
  smashed up Iraq see killed a lot of people
By for no known reason the we inflamed a whole region dawn's we inflamed
  a whole region early so misused light we smashed up Iraq
What The Star-Spangled Banner so like the flag proudly killed a lot of
  people we for no known reason hailed we smashed up Iraq
At like the flag the The Star-Spangled Banner twilight's for no known
  reason last we inflamed a whole region gleaming so misused

Whose killed a lot of people broad we inflamed a whole region stripes
  killed a lot of people and so misused bright like the flag stars The Star-
  Spangled Banner
Through we smashed up Iraq the for no known reason perilous for no
  known reason fight so misused
O'er like the flag the we inflamed a whole region ramparts The Star-
  Spangled Banner we we smashed up Iraq watched killed a lot of people
Were we inflamed a whole region so so misused gallantly The Star-
  Spangled Banner streaming for no known reason

And like the flag the we smashed up Iraq rocket's killed a lot of people red
  The Star-Spangled Banner glare we smashed up Iraq
The killed a lot of people bombs for no known reason bursting we inflamed
  a whole region in so misused air like the flag
Gave we smashed up Iraq proof we inflamed a whole region through so
  misused the like the flag night for no known reason
That killed a lot of people our The Star-Spangled Banner flag The Star-
  Spangled Banner was killed a lot of people still like the flag there for no
  known reason

O so misused say we smashed up Iraq does we inflamed a whole region that
for no known reason star we inflamed a whole region spangled like the
flag banner so misused yet killed a lot of people wave we smashed up Iraq
O'er The Star-Spangled Banner the we smashed up Iraq land so misused
of killed a lot of people the The Star-Spangled Banner free The Star-
Spangled banner
And so misused the like the flag home we smashed up Iraq of killed a lot of
people the for no good reason brave we inflamed a whole region

★

for Ornette Coleman (1930-2015)

O Ornette say freedom can reach you telling see doodles
By ringbearer the self dawn's pole early seething light holes
What hesitation so hellebore proudly ashen we lacked hailed Pam
At burl the milk twilight's cherry last sonogram gleaming horseshoe

Whose Pullman broad suspicions stripes Pigmeat and bilks bright ultimate
    stars Burgundy
Through imitation the instantaneous perilous bop fight find
O'er steam the bailiwick ramparts proke we eased watched ushers
Were bemistered so possible gallantly wrongdoing streaming benefits

And monetary the underground rocket's tongue red elbows glare Pomodoro
The color bombs bales bursting Turks in rancic air domes
Gave furtive proof assertive through dumdums the patience night image
That plumbs our imbricated flag Alvin was posted still tourist there Arno

O Ornette say freedom does Saenredam that hugs star Burma spangled
    Hopkins banner tentative yet meanering wave ruse
O'er humdrum the mace land quarreling of Dylan the bail free Gotham
And confident the hawk home Ballantine of Hillary the sequent
    brave tailgate

★

O Ornette say everything can pearldrops you limebakes see basketball
By Reece the easystreet dawn's funhouse early blamegame light stillborn
What purchases so hocks proudly poles we silted hailed flogged
At gravy the contingent twilight's slaphappy last dueling gleaming periwinkle

Whose periscopes broad logged stripes binocular and stereopticon bright
    panoptical stars hibernation
Through chestwounds the devious perilous rigor fight pusillanimity
O'er somnolent the Humpty-Dumpty ramparts tangential we sidelined
    watched relegated
Were pigeonholed so pearldrops gallantly pillowcase streaming ornaments

And ornithology the ricecakes rocket's temporary red elevator glare
    positron
The pell-mell bombs noggins bursting sausages in cricket air properties
Gave salvation proof hotdogs through demonstration the molybdenum
    night hijacking
That randy our intolerable flag dallaga was finitely still reassembled there
    enfant

O Ornette say everything does preening that breathing star dogshit
    spangled ombudsman banner Philadelphia yet telepathic wave Zeeland
O'er bobolink the Papadopoulos land magus of esplanade the bollixed free
    expression
And panjandrum the parallelogram home dominoes of Menander the
    pinecone brave crossing

Donald Trump at the Republican Debate
on August 6, 2015

O I cannot say say I'm leading by quite a bit can I want to win as the
    Republican you I will not make the pledge see only Rosie O'Donnell
By I've been challenged the I don't frankly have time dawn's and this country
    doesn't have time early this country is in big trouble light we don't win
    anymore
What we lose to China so we lose to Mexico proudly we lose to everybody we
    and honestly, Megyn hailed I've been very nice to you
At I could probably maybe not be the but I wouldn't do that twilight's Mexico is
    sending drugs last our money going out gleaming the drugs coming in

Whose we need to build a wall broad and I don't mind stripes a big beautiful
    door in that wall and our leaders are stupid bright the Mexican government
    is much smarter stars they send the bad ones over
Through as far as single payer the I have a big company perilous I have like
    one bidder fight you know why?
O'er because the insurance companies the they have control of the politicians
    ramparts they're making a fortune we we have to take care of people
    watched I will do that through a different system
Were most of the people on this stage so I've given to gallantly just so you
    understand streaming a lot of money

And I gave to many people the I was a businessman rocket's I give to everybody
    red when they call, I give glare and do you know what?
The when I need something bombs they are there for me bursting with Hillary
    Clinton in I said be at my wedding air and she came to my wedding
Gave you know why? proof she didn't have a choice through I gave to a
    foundation the I have used the laws of this country night for my company,
    my family
That I'm not going to name their names our they've used the law flag I have a
    great, great company was four times, I've taken advantage of the laws still
    these lenders aren't babies there I had the good sense to leave Atlantic City

O Chris can tell you say I made a lot of money in Atlantic City does I'm very
 proud of it that I've evolved on many issues star Ronald Reagan evolved
 spangled it was going to be aborted banner and it wasn't aborted yet
 that child today is a total superstar wave I would be so different
O'er from what you have right now the a president who doesn't have a
 clue land if Iran was a stock of you folks should go out and buy it the
 because you'll quadruple free we don't win anymore
And we don't beat China the we don't beat Japan home we can't beat
 Mexico of we can't do anything right the we have to make our country
 great again brave thank you

★

O The Star-Spangled Banner say blowing paydirt can position numbers you
    anguished card see eat its young
By pomegranate icing the stuttering bromide dawn's l'apresmidi early
    spaghetti dog light Zippo
What purple theorems so blared proudly branded X we oppressed hailed
    illegitimate time
At revulsion the handsome dolly twilight's pineapple surprise last ice
    house gleaming Seagull Brandy

Whose brandied pillow broad lashes leftward stripes in arrears and melted
    Helen bright banished Argyll stars abundant stars
Through oblivion sandwich the houseboat shot perilous risible ripples fight
    beyond pillboxes
O'er tangerine plains the stuttering lights ramparts disuniting states we
    solitary icecubes watched holistic basketball
Were telescoped dentures so insoluble breakfast gallantly polecat birthday
    streaming pileated hamburgers

And hotly pursued the stuttering arrow rocket's parallel petunias red
    billabong glare Hamburg express
The pointed alligator bombs and toiletbowls bursting illustrated husbandry
    in arena hack air in Moscow
Gave jellyroll membership proof hocking through Marlboro the boing
    brigade night pomaded hellcats
That indivisible poolroom our common boxcar flag oriole banter was
    ordained pipedream still passes fussbudget there elevates nemeses

O The Star-Spangled Banner say icy fountain does burn humdrum that
    pens Tupelo star Bellerophon fudge spangled orifice banner application
    handoff yet somatic popguns wave opportunistically
O'er barnstorming the pocketbook hollows land bought low of pentathlon
    penitentiary the stuttered assent free expectorating
And jilted doggies the stuttering barometer home under mint of corner
    crews the stuttering office brave not long

104

★

O America say America can America you America see America
By America the America dawn's America early America light America
What America so America proudly America we America hailed America
At America the America twilight's America last America gleaming America

Whose America broad America stripes America and America bright America
    stars America
Through America the America perilous America fight America
O'er America the America ramparts America we America watched America
Were America so America gallantly America streaming America

And America the America rocket's America red America glare America
The America bombs America bursting America in America air America
Gave America proof America through America the America night America
That America our America flag America was America still America there
    America

O America say America does America that America star America spangled
    America banner America yet America wave America
O'er America the America land America of America the America free America
And America the America home America of America the America brave
    America

Voices at the End of Election Night
on November 9, 2016

O It's the most disgusting thing I've ever seen. say Hoping for a miracle,
  you know? Can James Comey was the difference. you They worked that
  email thing—and it worked. see The Clintons did a bad job defending
  themselves.
By Oh my God, AP called Pennsylvania! the Boy, what a flop, huh? What a
  choke. dawn's This is a massive, incredible failure. early Getting hacked
  had a bit to do with it. light We've got Heineken, we've got Modelo.
What Beer's in the bucket, and wine's over there. so We're currently
  pouring a Chardonnay, and a Rioja…. proudly Free bar for the first
  hour, then cash bar after that. we Anybody wanna offer a toast? hailed
  They just gave Trump Wisconsin.
At We got beer, we got wine, bourbon. the Time to go. I'm getting sick of the
  world. twilight's Sick of life, you know? last This is the shit that death
  washes away. gleaming My daughter is really upset. She's, like, throwing up.

Whose Here's what I just wrote my daughters: broad Girls, now you know
  what real failure is. stripes What I felt in 1980, 1984, 1988, 2000 and
  2004. and This is worse. This is so worse. bright May things go better
  the in rest of our lives. stars You know what we died from, Dave?
Through I think we raise a glass to the most spectacular coverage the of
  the most amazing presidential election, perilous and we continue to
  drive this semi down the road night and change all the wheels at the
  same time.
O'er We've done amazing turns, we've made a difference. the And it's been
  a really, really wild ride. ramparts And I think that we all deserve a
  little tipple. we And we don't get to rest, watched because there's so
  much more to do,
Were but I think we can take a moment to reflect so on the fact that
  18 months ago, gallantly there was something like 18 Republican
  candidates, streaming and one of them was Donald Trump.

And And there was a coronation festival being held for Hillary Clinton. the And we've done a lot of real journalism, rocket's and real skepticism, and real cynicism, red and I know we fought hard on all of these stories all the way through. glare But I think all of us, and all of the reporters we worked with,

The we'll look back on it and say we did the right thing. bombs Because look what happened, right? bursting We weren't incredulous, and we weren't too credulous. in We walked down the middle path as much as we could, air and that was the right path to be on.

Gave So thank you all for helping get us this far, proof and for continuing to help us the rest of the way. Cheers! through You know the single thing we died from, Dave? the Bill Clinton getting on that fucking plane. night That prevented Loretta Lynch from stopping Comey.

That Comey. Weiner. Huma. Bill getting on the plane. our It's all in there. That's where the loss is. flag When Weiner blew up in the mayoral race, was I said, "You can't have people like them around you." still It's just like when Obama picked Comey, there I said, "We could end up dying from this."

O Hopefully people will realize what a terrible decision it is say and stop being such racist, sexist, homophobic, xenophobic assholes. does Is anyone calling cabs? I'm tempted to just flag one. that I don't even wanna go outside. star Bill Clinton getting on the plane, Dave. spangled Because Lynch could've blocked Comey otherwise. banner You're just gonna have to wait for the old white people to die. yet This isn't gonna last forever. Tell your daughters wave by the time they're our age, it'll be a lot different.

O'er So what was the killer, Dave? the President Elect Donald Trump. land You think Sanders would have beat him? of That's an interesting question. I'm not sure. the I don't think this country would elect somebody that liberal. free So, Dave, the killer? Not one thing?

And They're saying Trump's gonna speak soon. the OK, I gotta go. I just got to the end. home As Mike Pence comes on stage. of We're such fucking losers. We need better players. the It's time to call it quits brave and devote the rest of my life to poetry.

★

O failure say national can generational you personal see my
By your the his dawn's her early our light their
What failure so my proudly her we generational hailed national
At our the his twilight's personal last your gleaming failure

Whose failure broad their stripes generational and their bright your stars
    national
Through personal the our perilous his fight her
O'er my the national ramparts his we their watched generational
Were her so my gallantly your streaming failure

And failure the personal rocket's our red your glare his
The national bombs generational bursting her in personal air my
Gave failure proof their through our the her night your
That personal our national flag our was their still my there failure

O failure say personal does his that generational star her spangled national
    banner your yet his wave generational
O'er personal the their land my of our the our free personal
And my the your home her of his the generational brave failure

In the newsroom, Inauguration Day 2017

Michael Handler Ruby is the author of six other full-length poetry collections, including *At an Intersection* (Alef Books, 2002), *Window on the City* (BlazeVOX [books], 2006), *The Edge of the Underworld* (BlazeVOX, 2010), *Compulsive Words* (BlazeVOX, 2010), *American Songbook* (Ugly Duckling Presse, 2013) and *The Mouth of the Bay* (BlazeVOX, 2019). His trilogy in prose and poetry, *Memories, Dreams and Inner Voices* (Station Hill Press, 2012), includes ebooks *Fleeting Memories* (Ugly Duckling, 2008) and *Inner Voices Heard Before Sleep* (Argotist Online, 2011). He is also the author of the ebooks *Close Your Eyes* (Argotist, 2018) and *Titles & First Lines* (Mudlark, 2018), and five chapbooks with the Dusie Kollektiv. He co-edited Bernadette Mayer's collected early books, *Eating the Colors of a Lineup of Words* (Station Hill, 2015), and Mayer's and Lewis Warsh's prose collaboration *Piece of Cake* (Station Hill, 2020). A graduate of Harvard College and Brown University's writing program, he lives in Brooklyn and works as an editor of U.S. news and political articles at *The Wall Street Journal.*